THOUGHTS

ON

EDUCATIONAL TOPICS

AND

INSTITUTIONS.

BY

GEORGE S. BOUTWELL.

BOSTON:
PHILLIPS, SAMPSON AND COMPANY.
MDCCCLIX.

STEREOTYPED BY
HOBART AND ROBBINS, BOSTON.

To

THE TEACHERS OF MASSACHUSETTS,

WHOSE

ENLIGHTENED DEVOTION TO THEIR DUTIES

HAS

CONTRIBUTED EFFECTUALLY TO THE ADVANCEMENT OF LEARNING,

This Volume

IS RESPECTFULLY DEDICATED.

G. S. B.

CONTENTS.

THE INTRINSIC NATURE AND VALUE OF LEARNING, AND ITS INFLUENCE UPON LABOR.

[Lecture before the American Institute of Instruction.]

WORDS and terms have, to different minds, various significations; and we often find definitions changing in the progress of events. Bailey says learning is "skill in languages or sciences." To this, Walker adds what he calls "literature," and "skill in anything, good or bad." Dr. Webster enlarges the meaning of the word still more, and says, "Learning is the knowledge of principles or facts received by instruction or study; acquired knowledge or ideas in any branch of science or literature; erudition; literature; science; knowledge acquired by experience, experiment, or observation." Milton gives us a rhetorical definition in a negative form, which is of equal value, at least, with any authority yet cited. "And though a linguist," says Milton, "should pride himself to have all the tongues that Babel cleft the world into, yet if he have not studied the solid things in them, as well as the words and lexicons, he were nothing so much to be esteemed a learned man, as any yeoman or tradesman competently wise in his mother dialect only." — "Language is but the instrument conveying to us things useful to be known."

This is kindred to the saying of Locke, that "men of much reading are greatly learned, but may be little knowing." We must give to the term *learning* a broad definition, if we accept Milton's statement that its end "is to repair the ruins of our first parents by regaining to know God aright;" for this necessarily implies that we are to study carefully everything relating to the nature of our existence, to the spot and scene of our existence, with its mysterious phenomena, and its comparatively unexplained laws. And we must, moreover, always keep in view the personal relations and duties which the Creator has imposed upon the members of the human race. The knowledge of these relations and duties is one form of learning; the disposition and the ability to observe and practise these relations and duties, is another and a higher form of learning. The first is the learning of the theologian, the schoolman; the latter is the learning of the practical Christian. Both ought to exist; but when they are separated, we place things above signs, facts above forms, life above ideas. Law and justice ought always to be united; but when by error, or fraud, or usurpation, they are separated, we observe the forms of law, but we respect the principles of justice. This is a good illustration of the principles which guide to a true distinction in the forms of learning. Of all the definitions enumerated, we must give to the word *learning* the broadest signification. It is safe to accept the statement of the great poet, that a man may be acquainted with many languages, and yet not be learned; even as the apostle said he should become as sounding brass or a tinkling cymbal, if he had not charity, though he spoke with the tongues of men and angels. Learning includes, no doubt, a knowledge of the languages, the sciences, and all literature; but it includes also much else; and this much else may be more important than the enumerated branches. The term *learned* has been limited, usually, by exclusive application to the schoolmen; but it is a matter of doubt, especially in this country, upon the broad definition laid down, whether there is more learning in the schools, or out of them. This remark, if true, is no reflection upon the schools, but much in favor of the world. Those were dark ages when learning was confined to the schools; and, though we can never be too grateful for their existence, and the fidelity with which they preserved the knowledge of other days, that is surely a higher attainment in the life of the race, when the learning of the world exceeds the learning of the cloister, the school, and the college.

In a private conversation, Professor Guyot made a remark which seems to have a public value. "You give to your schools," said he, "credit that is really due to the world. Looking at America with the eye of an European, it appears to me that your world is doing more and your schools are doing less, in the cause of education, than you are inclined to believe." For one, though I ought, as much as any, to stand for the schools, I give a qualified assent to the truth of this observation. There is much learning among us which we cannot trace directly to the schools; but the schools have introduced and fostered a spirit which has given to the world the power to make itself learned. It is much easier to disseminate what is called the spirit of education, than it was to create that spirit, and preserve it when there were few to do it homage. For this we are indebted to the schools. Unobserved in the process of change, but happy in its results, the business of education is not now confined to professional teachers.

The greatest change of all has been wrought by

the attention given to female education, so that the mother of this generation is not compelled to rely exclusively upon the school and the paid teacher, public or private, but can herself, as the teacher ordained by nature, aid her children in the preparatory studies of life. This power does not often manifest itself in a regular system of domestic school studies and discipline, but its influence is felt in a higher home preparation, and in the exhibition of better ideas of what a school should be. And we may assume, with all due respect to our maternal ancestry, that this fact is a modern feature, comparatively, in American civilization. Female education has given rise to some excesses of opinion and conduct; but the world is entirely safe, especially the self-styled lords of creation, and may wisely advocate a system of general education without regard to sex, and leave the effect to those laws of nature and revelation which are to all and in all, and cannot permanently be avoided or disobeyed.

The number of educators has strangely increased, and they often appear where they might least be expected. We speak of the revival of education, and think only of the change that has taken place in the last twenty years in the appropriations of money, the style of school-houses, and the fitness of professional teachers for the work in which they are engaged; but these changes, though great, are scarcely more noteworthy than those that have occurred in the management of our shops, mills, and farms. When we write the sign or utter the sound which symbolizes *Teacher*, what figure, being, or qualities, are brought before us? We *should* see a person who, in the pursuit of knowledge, is self-moving, and, in the exercise of the influence which knowledge gives, is able to appreciate the qualities of others; and who, moreover, possesses enough of inventive power to devise means by which he can lead pupils, students, or hearers, in the way they ought to go. We naturally look for such persons in the lecture-room, the school, and the pulpit. And we find them there; but they are also to be found in other places. There are thousands of such men in America, engaged in the active pursuits of the day. They are farmers, mechanics, merchants, operatives. They do not often follow text-books, and therefor are none the worse, but much the better teachers. Insensibly they have taken on the spirit of the teacher and the school, and, apparently ignorant of the fact, are, in the quiet pursuits of daily life, leaders of classes following some great thought, or devoted to some practical investigation. And in one respect these teachers are of a higher order than *some* — not all, nor most — of our professional teachers. They never cease to be students. When a man or woman puts on the garb of the teacher, and throws off the garb of the student, you will soon find that person so dwindled and dwarfed, that neither will hang upon the shoulders. This happens sometimes in the school, but never in the world.

The last twenty-five years have produced two new features in our civilization, that are at once a cause and a product of learning. I speak of the Press, and of Associations for mutual improvement.

The newspaper press of America, having its centre in the city of New York, is more influential than the press of any other country. It may not be conducted with greater ability; though, if compared with the English press, the chief difference unfavorable to America is found in the character of the leading editorial articles. In enterprise, in telegraphic business, maritime, and political news and information, the press of the United States is not behind that of Great Britain.

It must, however, be admitted that a given subject is usually more thoroughly discussed in a single issue from the English press; but it is by no means certain that public questions are, upon the whole, better canvassed in England than in America. Indeed, the opposite is probably true. Our press will follow a subject day after day, with the aid of new thoughts and facts, until it is well understood by the reader. European ideas of journalism cannot be followed blindly by the press of America. The journalist in Europe writes for a select few. His readers are usually persons of leisure, if they have not always culture and taste; and the issue of the morning paper is to them what the appearance of the quarterly, heavy or racy, is to the cultivated American reader.

But the American journalist, whatever his taste may be, cannot afford to address himself to so small an audience. He writes literally for the million; for I take it to be no exaggeration to say that paragraphs and articles are often read by millions of people in America. This fact is an important one, as it furnishes a good test of the standard taste and learning of the people. Our press answers the demand which the people make upon it. The mass of newspaper readers are not, in a scholastic sense, well-educated persons. Newspaper writers do not, therefore, trouble themselves about the colleges with their professors, but they seek rather to gain the attention and secure the support of the great body of the people, who know nothing of colleges except through the newspapers. We have always been permitted to infer the intellectual and moral character of the audiences of Demosthenes, from the orations of Demosthenes; and may we not also infer the character of the American people, from the character of the press that they support? In a single issue may often be found an editorial article upon some question of present interest; a sermon, address, or speech, from a leading mind of the country or the world; letters from various quarters of the globe; extracts from established literary and scientific journals; original essays upon political, literary, scientific, and religious subjects; and items of local or general interest for all classes of readers. This product of the press, in quantity and quality, could not be distributed, week after week, and year after year, among an ignorant class of people. It could be accepted by intelligent, thinking, progressive minds only; and, as a fact necessarily coëxisting, we find the newspaper press equally essential to the best-educated persons among us. The newspaper press in America is a century and a half old; but its power does not antedate this century, and its growth has been chiefly within the last twenty-five years. What that growth has been may be easily seen by any one who will compare the daily sheet of the last generation with the daily sheet of this; and the future of the American press may be easily predicted by those who consider the progressive influences among us, of which the newspaper must always be the truest representative.

Within the same brief period of time it has become the fixed custom of the people to associate together for educational objects.

As a consequence, we have the lyceum for all, libraries for all, professional institutes and clubs for merchants, mechanics, and farmers, and, at last, free libraries and lectures for the operatives in the mills. Where these institutions can exist, there must be a high order of general learning; and where these institutions do exist, and are sustained, the learning of the people, whether high or low at any given moment, must be rapidly improved. Yet some of these agencies — lectures and libraries, for example — are not free from serious faults. It may seem rash and indefensible to criticize lectures upon the platform of the lecturer; but, as the audience can inflict whatever penalty they please upon the speaker, he will so far assume responsibility as to say that amusement is not the highest object of a single lecture, and when sought by managers as the desirable object of a whole course, the lecture-room becomes a theatre of dissipation; surely not so bad as other forms of dissipation, but yet so distinctly marked, and so pernicious in its influence, as to be comparatively unworthy of general support. Let it not, however, be inferred that wit, humor, and drollery even, are to be excluded from the lecture-room ; but they should always be employed as means by which information is communicated. Between lecturers equal in other respects, one with the salt of humor, native to the soil, should be preferred ; but it is a sad reflection upon public taste, when a person whose entire intellectual capital is wit, humor, or buffoonery, is preferred to men of solid learning. But it is a worse view of human nature, when men of real merit and worth depreciate themselves and lower the public taste, by attempting to do what, at best, they can have but ill success in, and what they would despise themselves for, were they to succeed completely. Shakspeare says of a jester:

> "This fellow 's wise enough to play the fool ;
> And to do that well, craves a kind of wit :
> *　*　*　*　*　*
> This is a practice
> As full of labor as a wise man's art :
> For folly, that he wisely shows, is fit ;
> But wise men, folly-fallen, quite taint their wit."

A kindred mental dissipation follows in the steps of progress, and demands aliment from our public libraries. In the selection of books there is a wide range, from the trashy productions of the fifth-rate novelist, to stately history and exact science. It is, however, to be assumed that libraries will not be established until they are wanted, and that the want will not be pressing until there is a taste for reading somewhat general. Where this taste exists, it is fair to assume that it is in some degree elevated. The direction, however, which the taste of any community is to take, after the establishment of a public library, depends, in a great degree, upon the selection of books for its shelves. Two dangers are to be avoided. The first, and greatest, is the selection of books calculated to degrade the morals or intellect of the reader. This danger is apparent, and to be shunned needs but to be seen. Books, of more or less intrinsic value, are so abundant and cheap, that common men must go out of their way to gather a large collection that shall not contain works of real merit. But the object should be to exclude all worthless and pernicious works, and meet and improve the public taste, by offering it mental food better than that to which it has been accustomed. The other danger is negative, rather than positive ; but, as books are comparatively worthless when they are not read, it becomes a matter of great moment to select such as will touch the public mind at a few points, at least. It is indeed possible, and, under the guidance of some persons, it would be natural, to encumber the shelves of a library with *good books* that might ever remain so, saving only the contributions made to mould and mice.

Now, if you will pardon a little more fault-finding, — which is, I confess, a quality without merit, or, as Byron has it,

> "A man must serve his time to every trade
> Save censure — critics all are ready made," —

I will hazard the opinion that the practice of establishing libraries in towns for the benefit of a portion of the inhabitants only is likely to prove pernicious in the end. To be sure, reading for some is better than reading for none; but reading for all is better than either. In Massachusetts there is a general law that permits cities and towns to raise money for the support of libraries; yet the legislature, in a few cases, has granted charters to library associations. With due deference, it may very well be suggested, that, where a spirit exists which leads a few individuals to ask for a charter, it would be better to turn this spirit into a public channel, that all might enjoy its benefits. And it will happen, generally, that the establishment of a public library will be less expensive to the friends of the movement, and the advantages will be greater; while there will be an additional satisfaction in the good conferred upon others.

We shall act wisely if we apply to books a maxim of the Greeks: "All things in common amongst friends." Under this maxim Cicero has enumerated, as principles of humanity, not to deny one a little running water, or the lighting his fire by ours, if he has occasion; to give the best counsel we are able to one who is in doubt or distress; which, says he, "are things that do good to the person that receives them, and are no loss or trouble to him that confers them." And he quotes, with approbation, the words of Ennius:

> "He that directs the wandering traveller
> Doth, as it were, light another's torch by his own;
> Which gives him ne'er the less of light, for that
> It gave another."

A good book is a guide to the reader, and a well-selected library will be a guide to many. And shall we give a little running water, and turn aside or choke up the streams of knowledge? light the evening torch, and leave the immortal mind unillumined? give free counsel to the ignorant or distressed, when he might easily be qualified to act as his own counsellor? In July 1856, Mr. Everett gave five hundred dollars toward a library for the High School in his native town of Dorchester; and in 1854 Mr. Abbott Lawrence gave an equal sum to his native town for the establishment of a public library. These are not large donations, if we consider only the amount of money given; but it is difficult to suggest any other equal appropriation that would be as beneficial, in a public sense. These donations are noble, because conceived in a spirit of comprehensive liberality. They are examples worthy of imitation; and I venture to affirm, there is not one of our New England towns that has not given to the world a son able to make a similar contribution to the cause of general learning. Is it too much to believe that a public library in a town will double the number of persons having a taste for reading, and consequently double the number of well-educated people? For, though we are not educated by mere reading, it is yet likely to happen that one who has a taste for books will also acquire habits of observation, study, and reflection.

Professional institutes and clubs also serve to increase the sum of general learning. They have thus far avoided the evil which has waited or fastened upon similar associations in Europe, — subserviency to political designs. Every profession or interest of labor has peculiar ideas and special purposes. These ideas and purposes may be wisely promoted by distinct organizations. Who can doubt the utility of associations of merchants, mechanics, and farmers? They furnish opportunities for the exchange of opinions, the exhibition of products, the dissemination of ideas, and the knowledge of improvements, that are thus wisely made the property of all. Knowledge begets knowledge. What is the distinguishing fact between a good school and a poor one? Is it not, that in a good school the prevailing public sentiment is on the side of knowledge and its acquisition? And does not the same fact distinguish a learned community from an ignorant community? If, in a village or city of artisans, each one makes a small annual contribution to the general stock of knowledge, the aggregate progress will be appreciable, and, most likely, considerable. If, on the other hand, each one plods by himself, the sum of professional knowledge cannot be increased, and is likely to be diminished.

The moral of the parable of the ten talents is eminently true in matters of learning. "Unto every one that hath shall be given, and he shall have abundance: but from him that hath not shall be taken away even that which he hath." We cannot conceive of a greater national calamity than an industrial population delving in mental sluggishness at unrelieved and unchanging tasks. The manufacture of pins was commenced in England in 1583, and for two hundred and fifty years she had the exclusive control of the trade; yet all that period passed away without improvement, or change in the process; while in America the business was revolutionized, simplified, and economized one-half, in the period of five years. In 1840 the valuation of Massachusetts was about three hundred millions of dollars; but it is certain that a large portion of this sum should have been set off against the constant impoverishment of the land, commencing with the settlement of the state, — the natural and unavoidable result of an ignorant system of farm labor. The revival of education in America was soon followed by a marked improvement in the leading industries of the people, and especially in the department of agriculture. The principle of association has not yet been as beneficial to the farmers as to the mechanics; but the former are soon to be compensated for the delay. With the exception of the business of discovering small planets, which seem to have been created for the purpose of exciting rivalry among a number of enthusiastic, well-minded, but comparatively secluded gentlemen, agricultural learning has made the most marked progress in the last ten years. But an agricultural population is professionally an inert population; and, therefore, as in the accumulation of John Jacob Astor's fortune, it was more difficult to take the first step than to make all the subsequent movements. Now, however, the principle of association is giving direction and force to the labors of the farmer; and it is easy for any person to draw to himself, in that pursuit, the results of the learning of the world.

Libraries and lectures for the operatives in the manufactories constitute another agency in the cause of general learning. The city of Lawrence, under the lead of well-known public-spirited gentlemen there, has the honor of introducing the system in America. A movement, to which this is kindred, was previously made in England; but that movement had for its object the education of the operatives in the simple elements of learning, and among the females in a knowledge of household duties. An English writer says: "Many employers have already established schools in connection with their manufactories. From many instances before us, we may take that of Mr. Morris, of Manchester, who has risen, himself, from the condition of a factory operative, and who has felt in his own person the disadvantages under which that class of workmen labor. He has introduced many judicious improvements. He has spent about one hundred and fifty pounds in ventilating his mills; and has established a library, coffee-room, class-room, weekly lectures, and a system of industrial training. The latter has been established for females, of whom he employs a great many. This class of girls generally go to the mills without any knowledge of household duties; they are taught in the schools to sew, knit," etc.

But, in the provision made at Lawrence for intellectual culture, it is assumed, very properly, that the operatives are familiar with the branches usually taught in the public schools. This could not be assumed of an English manufacturing population, nor, indeed, of any town population, considered as a whole. Herein America has an advantage over England. Our laborers occupy a higher standpoint intellectually, and in that proportion their labors are more effective and economical. The managers and proprietors at Lawrence were influenced by a desire to improve the condition of the laborers, and had no regard to any pecuniary return to themselves, either immediate or remote. And it would be a sufficient satisfaction to witness the growth of knowledge and morality, thereby elevating society, and rendering its institutions more secure.

These higher results will be accompanied, however, by others of sufficient importance to be considered. When we *hire*, or, what is, for this inquiry, the same thing, *buy* that commodity called *labor*, what do we expect to get? Is it merely the physical force, the animal life contained in a given quantity of muscle and bone? In ordinary cases we expect these, but in all cases we expect something more. We sometimes buy, and at a very high cost, too, what has, as a product, the least conceivable amount of manual labor in it, — a professional opinion, for example; but we never buy physical strength merely, nor physical strength at all, unless it is directed by some intellectual force. The descending stream has power to drive machinery, and the arm of the idiot has force for some mechanical service, but they equally lack the directing mind. We are not so unwise as to purchase the power of the stream, or the force of the idiot's arm; but we pay for its application in the thing produced, and we often pay more for the skill that has directed the power than for the power itself. The river that now moves the machinery of a factory in which many scores of men and women find their daily labor, and earn their daily bread, was employed a hundred years ago in driving a single set of mill-stones; and thus a man and boy were induced to divide their time lazily between the grist in the hopper and the fish under the dam.

The river's power has not changed ; but the inventive, creative genius of man has been applied to it, and new and astonishing results are produced. With man himself this change has been even greater. In proportion to the population of the country, we are daily dispensing with manual labor, and yet we are daily increasing the national production. There is more mind directing the machinery propelled by the forces of nature, and more mind directing the machinery of the human body. The result is, that a given product is furnished by less outlay of physical force. Formerly, with the old spinning-wheel and hand-loom, we put a great deal of bone and muscle into a yard of cloth ; now we put in very little. We have substituted mind for physical force, and the question is, which is the more economical ? Or, in other words, is it of any consequence to the employer whether the laborer is ignorant or intelligent ?

Before we discuss this point abstractly, let us notice the conduct of men. Is any one willing to give an ignorant farm laborer as much as he is ready to pay for the services of an intelligent man ? And if not, why the distinction ? And if an ignorant man is not the best man upon a farm, is he likely to be so in a shop or mill ? And if not, we see how the proprietors of factories are interested in elevating the standard of learning, in the mills and outside. But they are not singular in this. All classes of employers are equally concerned in the education of the laborer; for learning not only makes his labor more valuable to himself, but the market price of the product is generally reduced, and the change affects favorably all interests of society. This benefit is one of the first in point of time, and the one, perhaps, most appreciable of all which learning has conferred upon the laborer. As each laborer, with the same expenditure of physical force, produces a greater result, of course the aggregate products of the world are vastly increased, although they represent only the same number of laborers that a less quantity would have represented under an ignorant system.

The division of these products upon any principle conceivable leaves for the laborer a larger quantity than he could have before commanded; for, although the share of the wealthy may be disproportionate, their ability to consume is limited; and, as poverty is the absence or want of things necessary and convenient for the purposes of life, according to the ideas at the time entertained, we see how a laboring population, necessarily poor while ignorance prevails, is elevated to a position of greater social and physical comfort, as mind takes the place of brute force in the industries of the world. Learning, then, is not the result of social comfort, but social comfort is the product of intelligence, and increases or diminishes as intelligence is general or limited. It is not, however, to be taken as granted that each laborer's position corresponds or answers to the sum of his own knowledge. It might happen that an ignorant laborer would enjoy the advantages of a general culture, to which he contributed little or nothing; and it must of necessity also happen that an intelligent laborer, in the midst of an ignorant population, as in Ireland or India, for example, would be compelled to accept, in the main, the condition of those around him. But there is no evidence on the face of society now, or in its history, that an ignorant population, whether a laboring population or not, has ever escaped from a condition of poverty. And the converse of the proposition is undoubtedly true, that an intelligent laboring community will soon become a wealthy community. Learning is sure to produce wealth; wealth is likely to contribute to learning, but it does not necessarily produce it. Hence it follows that learning is the only means by which the poor can escape from their poverty.

In this statement it is assumed that education does not promote vice; and not only is this negative assumption true, but it is safe to assume, further, that education favors virtue, and that any given population will be less vicious when educated than when ignorant. This, I cannot doubt, is a general truth, subject, of course, to some exceptions.

The educational struggle in which the English people are now engaged has made distinct and tangible certain opinions and impressions that are latent in many minds. There has been an attempt to show that vice has increased in proportion to education. This attempt has failed, though there may be found, of course, in all countries, single facts, or classes of facts, that seem to sustain such an opinion.

Now, suppose this case, — and neither this case nor any similar one has ever occurred in real life, — but suppose crime to increase as a people were educated, though there should be no increase of population; would this fact prove that learning made men worse? By no means. Our answer is apparent on the face of the change itself. By education, the business and pecuniary relations and transactions of a people are almost indefinitely multiplied; and temptations to crime, especially to crimes against property, are multiplied in an equal ratio. Would person or property be better respected in New York or Boston, if the most ignorant population of the world could be substituted for the present inhabitants of those cities? The business nerves of men are frequently shocked by some unexpected defalcation, and short-sighted moralists, who lack faith, exclaim, "All this is because men know so much!" Such certainly forget that for every defaulter in a city there are hundreds of honest men, who receive and render justly unto all, and hold without check the fortunes of others. So Mr. Drummond argued in the British House of Commons against a national system of education, because what he was pleased to call *instruction* had not saved William Palmer and John Sadlier. But the truth in this matter is not at the bottom of a well; it is upon the surface. Where it is the habit of society generally to be ignorant, you will find it the necessity of that society to be poor; and where ignorance and poverty both abound, the temptations to crime are unquestionably few, but the power to resist temptation is as unquestionably weak. The absence of crime is owing to the absence of temptation, rather than to the presence of virtue. Such a condition of society is as near to real virtue as the mental weakness of the idiot is to true happiness.

Turning again to the discussion in the British Parliament of April, 1856, we are compelled to believe that some English statesmen are, in principle and in their ideas of political economy, where a portion of the English cotton-spinners were a hundred years ago. The cotton-spinners thought the invention of labor-saving machinery would deprive them of bread; and a Mr. Ball gravely argues that schools will so occupy the attention of children, that the farmers' crops will be neglected. I am inclined to give you his own words; and I have no doubt you will be in a measure relieved of the dulness of this essay, when you listen to what was actually cheered in the British Commons. Speaking of the resolutions in favor of a national system of instruction, Mr. Ball said: "It was important to consider what would be their bearing on the agricultural districts of the country. He had obtained a return from his own farm, and, supposing the principles advocated by the noble lord were adopted, the results would be perfectly fearful. The following was the return he had obtained from his agent: William Chapman, ten years a servant on his (Mr. Ball's) farm; his own wages thirteen shillings, besides a house; he had seven children, who earned nine shillings a week; making together twenty-two shillings a week. Robert Arbor, fifteen years on the farm; wages thirteen shillings a week, and a house; six children, who earned six shillings a week; making together nineteen shillings. John Stevens, thirty-three years a servant on the farm; his own wages fourteen shillings a week; he had brought up ten children, whose average earnings had been twelve shillings weekly, making together twenty-six shillings a week. Robert Carbon, twenty-two years a servant on the farm; wages thirteen shillings a week; having ten children, who earned ten shillings a week; making together twenty-three shillings a week. Thus it appeared that in these four families the fathers earned fifty-three shillings weekly, and the children thirty-seven shillings a week; so that the children earned something more than two-thirds of the amount of the earnings of the fathers. He would ask the house, if the fathers were to be deprived of the earnings of the children, how could they provide bread for them? It was perfectly impossible. They must either increase the parent's wages to the amount of the loss he thus sustained, or they must make it up to him from a rate. Then, again, those who were at all conversant with agriculture knew that if they deprived the farmer of the labor of children, agriculture could not be carried on. There was no machinery by which they could get the weeds out of the land." — *London Times.*

The light which this statement furnishes is not hid under a bushel. The argument deserves a more logical form, and I proceed gratuitously to give the author the benefit of a scientific arrangement. "If a national system of education is adopted, the children of my tenants will be sent to school; if the children of my tenants are sent to school, my turnips will not be weeded; if my turnips are not weeded, I shall eat fat mutton no more."

After this from a statesman, we need not wonder that a correspondent of Lord John Russell writes, "That a farmer near him has been heard to say, he would not give anything to a day-school; he finds that since Sunday-schools have been established the birds have increased and eat his corn, and because he cannot now procure the services of the boys, whom he used to employ the whole of Sunday, in protecting his fields." —*London Times, April 13th,* 1856.

Now, I do not go to England for the purpose of making an attack upon her opinions; but, as kindred ideas prevail among us, though to a limited extent only, the folly of them may be seen in persons at a distance, when it would not be realized by ourselves. Moreover, the presentation of these somewhat ridiculous notions brings ridicule upon a whole class of errors; and when errors are so ingrained that men cannot reason in regard to them, ridicule is often the only weapon of successful attack. And it is no compliment to an American audience for the speaker to say that their own minds already suggest the refutation which these errors demand. If the chief end of man, for which boyhood should be a preparation, were to weed turnips or to frighten blackbirds from corn-fields, then surely the objection of Mr. Ball, and the complaint and spirit of resistance offered by Lord John Russell's farmer, would be eminently proper. But Lord John Russell did not himself assent to the view furnished by his correspondent. Mr. Ball's theory evidently is, "Take good care of the turnips, and leave the culture of the boys and girls to chance;" and Lord John Russell's wise farmer unquestionably thinks that cereal peculations of blackbirds are more dangerous than the robberies committed by neglected children, grown to men.

Mr. Clay, chaplain of Preston jail, says: "Thirty-six per cent. come into jail unable to say the Lord's Prayer; and seventy-two per cent. come in such a state of moral debasement that it is in vain to give them instruction, or to teach them their duty, since they cannot understand the meaning of the words used to them." Here we have, as cause and effect, the philosophy of Mr. Ball, and the facts of Mr. Clay. And, further, this philosophy is as bad in principle, when tried by the rules of political economy, as when subjected to moral and Christian tests.

Mr. Ball says there is no machinery by which the farmers can get the weeds out of the land. This may be true; and once there was no machinery by which they could get the seed into the land, or the crops from it. Once there was little or no inventive power among the mechanics, or scientific knowledge, or even spirit of inquiry, among the farmers. How have these changes been wrought? By education, surely, and that moral and religious culture for which secular education is a fit preparation. The contributions of learning to labor, in a pecuniary aspect alone, have far exceeded the contributions of labor to learning.

It is impossible to enumerate the evidences in support of this statement, but single facts will give us some conception of their aggregated value and force.

It was stated by Mr. Flint, Secretary of the Massachusetts Board of Agriculture, in his Annual Report for 1855, "That the saving to the country, from the improvements in ploughs alone, within the last twenty-five years, has been estimated at no less than ten millions of dollars a year in the work of teams, and one million in the price of ploughs, while the aggregate of the crops is supposed to have been increased by many millions of bushels." From this fact, as the representative of a great class of facts, we may safely draw two conclusions. First, these improvements are the products of learning, the contribution which learning makes to labor, far exceeding in amount any tax which the cause of learning, in schools or out, imposes upon labor. Secondly, we see that a given amount of adult labor upon a farm, with the help of the improved implements of industry, will accomplish more in 1856, than the same amount of adult labor, with its attendant juvenile force, could have accomplished in 1826. If we were fully to illustrate and sustain the latter inference, we should be required to review the improvements made in other implements of farming, as well as in ploughs. Their positive pecuniary value, when considered in the aggregate, is too vast for general belief; and in England alone it must exceed the anticipated cost of a system of public instruction, say six millions of pounds, or thirty millions of dollars, per year. But learning, as we have defined it, has contributed less to farming than to other departments of labor.

The very existence of manufactures presupposes the existence of learning. There is no branch of manufactures without its appropriate machine; and every machine is the product of mind, enlarged and disciplined by some sort of culture. The steam engine, the spinning-jenny, the loom, the cotton-gin, are notable instances of the advantages derived by manufacturing industry from the prevalence of learning. It was stated by Chief Justice Marshall, about thirty years ago, that Whitney's cotton-gin had saved five hundred millions of dollars to the country; and the saving, upon the same basis, cannot now be less than one thousand millions of dollars, — a sum too great for the human imagination to conceive. When we contemplate these achievements of mind, by which manual labor has been diminished, and every physical force both magnified and economized, how unstatesmanlike is the view which regards a human being as a bundle of muscles and bones merely, with no destiny but ignorance, servitude, and poverty!

Ancient commerce, if we omit to notice the conjecture that the mariner's compass was in possession of the old Phœnician and Indian navigators, reproduced, rather than invented, in modern times, did not rest upon any enlarged scientific knowledge; but, in this era, many of the sciences contribute to the extension and prosperity of trade. After what has been accomplished by science, and especially by physical geography, for commerce and navigation, we have reason to expect a system, based upon scientific knowledge and principles, which shall render the highway of nations secure against the disasters that have often befallen those who go down to the sea in ships. Science gave to the world the steamship, which promised for a time to engross the entire trade upon the ocean; but science again appears, constructs vessels upon better scientific principles, traces out the path of currents in the water and the air, and thus restores the rival powers of wind and steam to an equality of position in the eye of the merchant. Will any one say that all this inures to capital, and leaves the laborer comparatively unrewarded? We are accustomed to use the word prosperity as synonymous with accumulation; and yet, in a true view, a man may be prosperous and accumulate nothing. Suppose we contrast two periods in the life of a nation with each other. Since the commencement of this century, the wages of a common farm laborer in America have increased seventy-five or one hundred per cent., while the articles necessary and convenient for his use have, upon the whole, diminished in price. Admit that there was nothing for accumulation in the first period, and that there is nothing for accumulation now, — is not his condition nevertheless improved? And, if so, has he not participated in the general prosperity?

Indeed, we may all accept the truth, that there is no exclusiveness in the benefits which learning confers; and this leads me to say, next, that there ought to be no exclusiveness in the enjoyment of educational privileges.

In America we agree to this ; and yet, confessedly, as a practical result we have not generally attained the end proposed. There are two practical difficulties in the way. First, our aim in a system of public instruction is not high enough ; and, secondly, we do not sufficiently realize the importance of educating each individual. Our aim is not high enough ; and the result, like every other result, is measured and limited by the purpose we have in view. Our public schools ought to be so good that private schools for instruction in the ordinary branches would disappear. Mr. Everett said, in reply to inquiries made by Mr. Twistleton, "I send my boy to the public school, because I know of none better." It should be the aim of the public to make their schools so good that no citizen, in the education of his children, will pass them by.

It is as great a privilege for the wealthy as for the poor to have an opportunity to send their children to good public schools. It is a maxim in education that the teacher must first comprehend the pupil mentally and morally ; and might not many of the errors of individual and public life be avoided, if the citizen, from the first, were to have an accurate idea of the world in which he is to live? The demand of labor upon education, as they are connected with every material interest of society, is, that no one shall be neglected. The mind of a nation is its capital. We are accustomed to speak of money as capital; and sometimes we enlarge the definition, and include machinery, tools, flocks, herds, and lands. But for this moment let us do what we have a right to do, — go behind the definitions of lexicographers and political economists, and say, "*capital* is the producing force of society, and that force is mind." Without this force, money is nothing; machinery is nothing; flocks, herds, lands, are nothing. But all these are made valuable and efficient by the power of mind. What we call civilization, — passing from an inferior to a superior condition of existence, — is a mental and moral process. If mind is the capital, — the producing force of society, — what shall we say of the person or community that neglects its improvement? Certainly, all that we should say of the miser, and all that was said of the timid servant who buried his talent in the earth. If one mind is neglected, then we fail as a generation, a state, a nation, as members of the human family, to answer the highest purposes of existence. Some possible good is unaccomplished, some desirable labor is unperformed, some means of progress is neglected, some evil seed, it may be, is sown, for which this generation must answer to all the successions of men. But let us not yield to the prejudice, though sanctioned by custom, that learning unfits men for the labors of life. The *schools* may sometimes do this, but *learning* never. We cannot, however, conceal from our view the fact that this prejudice is a great obstacle to progress, even in New England; an obstacle which may not be overcome without delay and conflict, in many states of this Union; and especially in Great Britain is it an obstacle in the way of those who demand a system of universal education.

In the House of Commons, Mr. Drummond opposes a national system of education in this wise: "And, pray, what do you propose to rear your youth for? Are you going to train them for statesmen? No. (A laugh.) The honorable gentleman laughs at the notion, and so would I. But you are going to fit them to be — what? Why, cotton-spinners and pin-makers, or, if you like, blacksmiths, mere day laborers. These are the men whom you are to teach foreign languages, mathematics, and the notation of music. (Hear, hear.) Was there ever anything more absurd? It really seems as if God had withdrawn common sense from this house." Now, what does this language of Mr. Drummond mean? Does he not intend to say that it is unwise to educate that class of society from which cotton-spinners, pin-makers, blacksmiths, mere day laborers, are taken? Is it not his opinion that the business of pin-making is to be perpetuated in some families and classes, and the business of statesmanship is to be perpetuated in others? And, if so, does he not believe that the best condition of society is that which presents divisions based upon the factitious distinctions of birth and fortune? Most certainly these questions indicate his opinions, as they indicate the opinions of those who cheered him, and as they also indicate the opinions of a few in this country, who, through ignorance, false education, prejudice, or sympathy with castes and races, fear to educate the laborer, lest he may forsake his calling. With us these fears are infrequent, but they ought not to exist at all. The question in a public sense is not, "From what family or class shall the pin-maker or the statesman be taken?" There is no question at all to be answered. Educate the whole people. Education will develop every variety of talent, taste, and power. These qualities, under the guidance of the necessities of life and the public judgment, will direct each man to his proper place. If the son of a cotton-spinner become a statesman, it is because statesmanship needs him, and he has some power answering to its wants. And if Mr. Drummond's son become a cotton-spinner, it is because that is his right place, and the world will be the better and the richer that Mr. Drummond's son is a cotton-spinner, and that he is a learned man too; but, if Mr. Drummond's son occupy the place of a statesman because he is Mr. Drummond's son, though he be no statesman at all himself, then the world is all the worse for the mistake, and poor compensation is it that Mr. Drummond's son is a learned man in something that he is never called to put in practice.

When it is said that the statesmen, or those engaged in the business of government, shall come from one-tenth of the population, is not the state, according to the doctrine of chances, deprived of nine-tenths of its governing force? And may not the same suggestion be made of every other branch of business?

But I pass now to the last leading thought, and soon to the conclusion of my address. The great contribution of learning to the laborer is its power, under the lead of Christianity, to break down the unnatural distinctions of society, and to render labor of every sort, among all classes, acceptable and honorable. Ignorance is the degradation of labor, and when laborers, as a class, are ignorant, their vocation is necessarily shunned by some; and, being shunned by some, it is likely to be despised by others. Wherever the laboring population is in a condition of positive, or, by a broad distinction, of comparative ignorance, society will always divide itself into two, and oftentimes into three classes. We shall find the dominant class, the servient class, and then, generally, the despised class; the dominant class, comparatively intelligent, possessing the property, administering the government, giving to social life its laws, and enjoying the fruits of labor which they do not perform; the servient class, unwittingly in a state of slavery, whether nominally bond or free, having little besides physical force to promote their own comfort or to contribute to the general prosperity, and furnishing security in their degradation for a final submission to whatever may be required of them; and last, a despised class, too poor to live without labor, and too proud to live by labor, assuming a position not accorded to them, and finally yielding to a social and political ostracism even more degrading, to a sensitive mind, than the servient condition they with so much effort seek to shun.

All this is the fruit of ignorance; all this may be removed by general learning. If all men are learned, the work of the world will be performed by learned men; and why, under such circumstances, should not every vocation that is honest be equally honorable? But if this, in a broad view, seem utopian, can we not agree that learning is the only means by which a poor man can escape from his poverty? And, if it furnish certain means of escape for one man, will it not furnish equally certain means of escape for many? And if so, is not learning a general remedy for the inequalities among men?

EDUCATION AND CRIME.

[Extract from the Twenty-First Annual Report of the Secretary of the Massachusetts Board of Education.]

The public schools, in their relations to the morals of the pupils and to the morality of the community, are attracting a large share of attention. In some sections of the country the system is boldly denounced on account of its immoral tendencies. In states where free schools exist there are persons who doubt their utility; and occasionally partisan or religious leaders appear who deny the existence of any public duty in regard to education, or who assert and maintain the doctrine that free schools are a common danger. As the people of this commonwealth are not followers of these prophets of evil, nor believers in their predictions, there is but slight reason for discussion among us. It is not probable that a large number of the citizens of Massachusetts entertain doubts of the power and value of our institutions of learning, of every grade, to resist evil and promote virtue, through the influence they exert. But, as there is nothing in our free-school system that shrinks from light, or investigation even, I have selected from the annual reports everything which they contain touching the morality of the institution. In so doing, I have had two objects in view. First, to direct attention to the errors and wrongs that exist; and, secondly, to state the opinion, and enforce it as I may be able, that the admitted evils found in the schools are the evils of domestic, social, municipal, and general life, which are sometimes chastened, mitigated, or removed, but never produced, nor even cherished, by our system of public instruction. In the extracts from the school committees' reports there are passages which imply some doubt of the moral value of the system; but it is our duty to bear in mind that these reports were prepared and presented for the praiseworthy purpose of arousing an interest in the removal of the evils that are pointed out. The writers are contemplating the importance of making the schools a better means of moral and intellectual culture; but there is no reason to suppose that in any case a comparison is instituted, even mentally, between the state of society as it appears at present and the condition that would follow the abandonment of our system of public instruction. There are general complaints that the manners of children and youth have changed within thirty or fifty years; that age and station do not command the respect which was formerly manifested, and that some license in morals has followed this license in manners.

The change in manners cannot be denied ; but the alleged change in morals is not sustained by a great amount of positive evidence. The customs of former generations were such that children often manifested in their exterior deportment a deference which they did not feel, while at present there may be more real respect for station, and deference for age and virtue, than are exhibited in juvenile life. In this explanation, if it be true, there is matter for serious thought ; but I should not deem it wise to encourage a mere outward show of the social virtues, which have no springs of life in the affections.

And, notwithstanding the tone of the reports to which I have called attention, and notwithstanding my firm conviction that many moral defects are found in the schools, I am yet confident that their moral progress is appreciable and considerable.

In the first place, teachers, as a class, have a higher idea of their professional duties, in respect to moral and intellectual culture. Many of them are permanently established in their schools. They are persons of character in society, with positions to maintain, and they are controlled by a strong sense of professional responsibility to parents and to the public. It has been, to some extent, the purpose and result of Teachers' Associations, Teachers' Institutes, and Normal Schools, to create in the body of teachers a better opinion concerning their moral obligations in the work of education. It must also be admitted that the changes in school government have been favorable to learning and virtue. For, while it is not assumed that all schools are, or can be, controlled by moral means only, it is incontrovertible that a government of mild measures is superior to one of force. This superiority is as apparent in morals as in scholarly acquisitions. It is rare that a teacher now boasts of his success over his pupils in physical contests; but such claims were common a quarter of a century ago. The change that has been wrought is chiefly moral, and in its influence we find demonstrative evidence of the moral superiority of the schools of the present over those of any previous period of this century. Before we can comprehend the moral work which the schools have done and are doing, we must perceive and appreciate with some degree of truthfulness the changes that have occurred in general life within a brief period of time. The activity of business, by which fathers have been diverted from the custody and training of their children; the claims of fashion and society, which have led to some neglect of family government on the part of mothers; the aggregation of large populations in cities and towns, always unfavorable to the physical and moral welfare of children; the comparative neglect of agriculture, and the consequent loss of moral strength in the people, are all facts to be considered when we estimate the power of the public school to resist evil and to promote good. If, in addition to these unfavorable facts and tendencies, our educational system is prejudicial to good morals, we may well inquire for the human agency powerful enough to resist the downward course of New England and American civilization. To be sure, Christianity remains; but it must, to some extent, use human institutions as means of good; and the assertion that the schools are immoral is equivalent to a declaration that our divine religion is practically excluded from them. This declaration is not in any just sense true. The duty of daily devotional exercises is always inculcated upon teachers, and the leading truths and virtues of Christianity are made, as far as possible, the daily guides of teachers and pupils. The tenets of particular sects are not taught; but the great truths of Christianity, which are received by Christians generally, are accepted and taught by a large majority of committees and teachers. It is not claimed that the public schools are religious institutions ; but they recognize and inculcate those fundamental truths which are the basis of individual character, and the best support of social, religious, and political life. The statement that the public schools are demoralizing must be true, if true at all, for one of three reasons. Either because all education is demoralizing ; or, secondly, because the particular education given in the public schools is so ; or, thirdly, because the public-school system is corrupting, and consequently taints all the streams of knowledge that flow through or emanate from it. For, if the public system is unobjectionable as a system, and education is not in itself demoralizing, then, of course, no ground remains for the charge that I am now considering.

I. *Is all education demoralizing?* An affirmative answer to this question implies so much that no rational man can accept it. It is equivalent to the assertion that barbarism is a better condition than civilization, and that the progress of modern times has proceeded upon a misconception of the true ideal perfection of the human race. As no one can be found who will admit that his happiness has been marred, his powers limited, or his life degraded, by education, so there is no process of logic that can commend to the human understanding the doctrine that bodies of men are either less happy or virtuous for the culture of the intellect. I am not aware of any human experience that conflicts with this view; for individual cases of criminals who have been well educated prove nothing in themselves, but are to be considered as facts in great classes of facts which indicate the principles and conduct of bodies of men who are subject to similar influences. In fact, the statistics to which I have had access tend to show that crime diminishes as intelligence increases. On this point the experience of Great Britain is probably more definite, and, of course, more valuable, than our own. The Aberdeen Feeding Schools were established in 1841, and during the ten years succeeding the commitments to the jails of children under twelve years of age were as follows: *

In 1842,	30	In 1847,	27
1843,	63	1848,	19
1844,	41	1849,	16
1845,	49	1850,	22
1846	28	1851,	8
	211		92

In the work of Mr. Hill it is also stated that "the number of children under twelve committed for

* The Repression of Crime. By M. D. Hill.

crime to the Aberdeen prisons, during the last six years, was as follows :

	Males.	Females.	Total.
1849–50,	11	5	16
1850–51,	14	8	22
1851–52,	6	2	8
1852–53,	23	1	24
1853–54,	24	1	25
1854–55,	47	2	49

"It will be observed that in the last three years there has been a great increase of boy crime, contemporaneously with an almost total absence of girl crime, though formerly the amount of the latter was considerable. Now, since this extraordinary difference coïncides in point of time with the fact of full girls' schools and half empty boys' schools, the inference can hardly be avoided that the two facts bear the relation of cause and effect, and that, so far from the late increase of youthful crime in Aberdeen anywise impairing the soundness of the principle on which the schools are based, it is its strongest confirmation. In moral as in physical science, when the objections to a theory are, upon further investigation, explained by the theory itself, they become the best evidence of its truth. Indeed, it is proved, by the experience, not only of Aberdeen, but, as far as I have been able to ascertain, of every town in Scotland in which industrial schools have been established, that the number of children in the schools and the number in the jail are like the two ends of a scale-beam; as the one rises the other falls, and *vice versa.*

"The following list of imprisonments of children attending the schools of the Bristol Ragged School Union shows considerable progress in the right direction:

	1847.	1848.	1849.	1850.	1851.	1852.	1853.	1854.	1855.
Imprisoned,	12	19	26	9	1	1	–	1	–

Imprisonments in the first four years, } 66, averaging 16.5 per year on number of 417 children.

In subsequent five years, } 3, averaging 0.6 per year on number of 728 children.

Difference, ... 15.9

16.5 : 15.9 : : 100 : 96.36.

"Thus," says Mr. Thornton, "it appears that the diminution of the average annual number of children attending our schools imprisoned in the latter period of five years, as compared with the annual average of the previous four years, is ninety-six per cent. — a striking fact, which is, I think, a manifest proof of the benefit conferred on them by the religious and secular instruction they receive in our schools, or, at the very least, of the advantages of rescuing them from the temptations of idleness, and from evil companionship and example."

I also copy, from the work already referred to, an extract from a paper on the Reformatory Institutions in and near Bristol, by Mary Carpenter: "In numberless instances children may be seen growing up decently, who owe their only training and instruction to the school. Young persons are noticed in regular work, who, before they attended the Ragged Schools, were vagrants, or even thieves. Not unfrequently a visit is paid at the school by a respectable young man, who proves to have been a wild and troublesome scholar of former times."

Mr. Hill, Recorder of Birmingham, in a charge to the grand jury, made in 1839, speaking of the means of repressing crime, says: "It is to education, in the large and true meaning of the word, that we must all look as the means of striking at the root of the evil. Indeed, of the close connection between ignorance and crime the calendar which I hold in my hand furnishes a striking example. Each prisoner has been examined as to the state of his education, and the result is set down opposite his name. It appears, then, that of forty-three prisoners only one can read and write well. The majority can neither read nor write at all; and the remainder, with the solitary exception which I have noted down, are said to read and write imperfectly; which necessarily implies that they have not the power of using those great elements of knowledge for any practical object. Of forty-three prisoners, forty-two, then, are destitute of instruction."

These authorities are not cited because they refer to schools that answer in character to the public schools of Massachusetts, for the latter are far superior in the quality of their pupils, and in the opportunities given for intellectual and moral education; but these cases and opinions are presented for the purpose of showing what has been done for the improvement of children and the repression of crime under the most unfavorable circumstances that exist in a civilized community. If such benign results have followed the establishment of schools of an inferior character, is it unreasonable to claim that education and the processes of education, however imperfect they may be, are calculated to increase the sum of human progress, virtue, and happiness?

II. *Is the particular education given in the public schools unfavorable to the morals of the pupils, and, consequently, to the morality of the community?* I have already presented a view of the moral and religious education given in the schools, and it only remains to consider the culture that is in its leading features intellectual. It may be said, speaking generally, that education is a training and development of the faculties, so as to make them harmonize in power, and in their relations to each other. Among other things, the ability to read is acquired in the public schools. In the individual, this is a power for good. It opens to the mind and heart the teachings of the sacred Scriptures; it secures the companionship of the great, the wise, and the good, of every age; and it is a possession that, in all cases, must be the foundation of those scientific acquisitions, intellectual, moral, and natural, which show the beneficence and power of the Creator, and indicate the fact and the law of human responsibility. The natural and general effect of the sciences taught in the schools is an illustration of the last statement. Moreover, the mere presence of a child, though he took no part in the studies of the school, is to him a moral lesson. He feels the force of government, he acquires the habit of obedience, and, in time, he comprehends the reason of the rules that are established. This discipline is essentially moral, and furnishes some basis, though partial and unsatisfactory, for the proper discharge of the duties of life. But it is to be remembered that the power of the school is but in its beginning when the presence of a pupil is recognized. The constancy and punctuality of attendance required by all judicious parents and faithful teachers are important moral lessons, whose influence can never be destroyed. The fixedness of purpose that is required, and is essential in school, remains as though it were a part of the nature of the child and the man. School-life strengthens habits of industry when they exist, and creates them when they do not. It is, indeed, the only means, of universal application, that is competent to train children in habits of industry. Private schools can never furnish this training; for large numbers of children, by the force of circumstances, are deprived of the tuition of such schools. Business life cannot furnish this training; for the habits of the child are usually moulded, if not hardened, before he arrives at an age when he can be constantly employed in any industrial vocation. The public school is no doubt justly chargeable with neglects and omissions; but its power for good, measured by the character of the education now furnished, is certainly very great. It inculcates habits of regularity, punctuality, constancy, and indústry, in the pursuits of business; through literature and the sciences in their elements, and, under some circumstances, by an advanced course of study, it leads the pupil towards the fountain of life and wisdom; and, by the moral and religious instruction daily given, some preparation is made for the duties of life and the temptations of the world.

III. *Is the public-school system, as a system, in itself necessarily corrupting?* As preliminary to the answer to be given to this question, it is well to consider what the public-school system is.

1. Every inhabitant is required to contribute to its support.

2. It contemplates the education of every child, regardless of any distinction of society or nature.

3. The system is subject in many respects to the popular will; and ultimately its existence and character are dependent upon the public judgment.

4. In the Massachusetts schools, the daily reading of the Scriptures is required.

The consideration of these topics will conclude my remarks upon the general subject of the moral influence of the American system of public instruction: In New England it is very unusual to hear the right of the state to provide for the support of schools by general taxation called in question; but I am satisfied, from private conversations, and from occasional public statements, that there are leading minds in some sections of the country that are yet unconvinced of the moral soundness of the basis on which a system of public instruction necessarily rests. Taxation is simply an exercise of the right of the whole to take the property of an individual; and this right can be exercised justly in those cases only where the application of the property so taken is, morally speaking, to a public use. The judgment of the public determines the legality of the proceeding; but it is possible that in some cases a public judgment might be secured which could not be supported by a process of moral reasoning. On what moral grounds, then, does the right of taxation for educational objects rest? I answer, first, education diminishes crime. The evidence in support of this statement has already been presented. It is a manifest individual duty to make sacrifices for this object; and, as every crime is an injury, not only to him who is the subject of it, but to every member of society, the prevention of crime becomes a public as well as an individual duty.

The conviction of a criminal is a public duty; and, under all governments of law, it is undertaken at the public charge. Offences are not individual merely; they are against society also, inasmuch as it is the right of society that all its members shall behave themselves well. And, if it is the right of society that its members shall behave themselves well, is it not the duty of society to so provide for their education that each individual part may meet the demand which the whole body asserts? And, further, as a majority of persons cannot individually provide for their own protection, it is the duty of society, or the state, or the government, to furnish the needed protection in the most economical and effective manner possible. The state has no moral right to jeopard property, life, and reputation, when, by a different policy, all these might be secure; nor has the state a moral right to make the security furnished, whether perfect or not, unnecessarily expensive. It is the dictate of reason and the experience of governments that the most effectual method of repressing crime is to diminish the number of criminals; and, though punitive measures may accomplish something, our chief reliance must be upon the education and training of children and youth. The facts drawn from the experience of England and Scotland, which have been quoted, lead to the conclusion that schools diminish the number of criminals, and consequently lessen the amount of crime; but I think it proper to add some extracts from a communication made, in August, 1856, by Mr. Dunne, chief constable of Newcastle-upon-Tyne, to the Secretary of the National Reformatory Union.*

"I know, from my own personal knowledge and

* The Repression of Crime, pp. 358, 359.

observation, that, since parental responsibility has been enforced in the district, under the direction of the Secretary of State, the number of juvenile criminals in the custody of the police has decreased one-half. I know that many of the parents, who were in the habit of sending their children into the streets for the purposes of stealing, begging, and plunder, have quite discontinued that practice, and several of the children so used, and brought up as thieves and mendicants, are now at some of the free schools of the town; others are at work, and thereby obtain an honest livelihood; and, so far as I can ascertain, they seem to be thoroughly altered, and appear likely to become good and honest members of society. I have, for my own information, conversed with some of the boys so altered, and, during the conversation I had with them, they declared that they derived the greatest happiness and satisfaction from their change in life. I don't at all doubt the truth of these statements, for their evident improvement and individual circumstances fully bear them out; and I believe them to be really serious in all they say, and truly anxious to become honest and respectable. I attribute, in a great measure, this salutary change to the effects arising in many respects from the establishment of reformatory schools; but I have more particularly found that greater advantages have emanated from those institutions since the parents of the children confined in them have been made to pay contributions to their maintenance ; for it appears beyond doubt that the effect of the latter has been to induce the parents of other young criminals to withdraw them from the streets, and, instead of using them for the purposes of crime, they seem to take an interest in their welfare. And I know that many of them are now really anxious to get such employment for their children as will enable them to obtain a livelihood ; and it is my opinion that the example thus set to older and more desperate criminals, belonging in many instances to the same family as the juvenile thief, has had the effect of reforming them also ; for many of them have left off their course of crime, and are now living by honest labor. The result is that serious crime has considerably decreased in this district, so much so that there were only six cases for trial at the assizes, whereas, at the previous assizes, the average number of cases was from twenty-five to thirty, which fact was made the subject of much comment and congratulation by Mr. Justice Willes, the presiding judge."

These remarks relate chiefly to the reformatory schools, but we know that the prevention of crime by education is much easier than its reformation by the same means. Indeed, it is the result of the experience of Massachusetts that the necessity for reform schools has in a large degree arisen from neglect of the public schools. It is stated in the Tenth Annual Report of the Chaplain of the State Reform School that of nineteen hundred and nine boys admitted since the establishment of the institution, thirteen hundred and thirty-four are known to have been truants. It is also quite probable that the number reported as truants is really less than the facts warrant. It may not be out of place to suggest, in this connection, that when a boy sentenced to the Reform School is known to have been guilty of truancy, if the parents were subjected to some additional burdens on that account, the cause of education would be promoted, and the number of criminals in the community would be diminished. From the views and facts presented, as well as from the daily observation and experience of men, I assume that ignorance is the ally of crime, and that education is favorable to virtue. It is also the result of experience and the dictate of reason that general taxation is the only means by which universal education can be secured. All other plans and theories will prove partial in their application. If, then, it is the duty of the state to protect itself against crime, and of course to diminish the number of criminals;

if education is the most efficient means for securing these results ; if this education must be universal in order to be thoroughly effective ; if the state is the only agent or instrumentality of sufficient power to establish schools and furnish education for all ; and if general taxation is the only means which the state itself can command, is not every inhabitant justly required and morally bound to contribute to the support of a system of public instruction ?

It will not necessarily happen that public schools will furnish to every child and youth the desired amount of education. Professional schools, classical schools, and academies of various grades, will be continued ; but there is an amount of intellectual and moral training needed by every child which can be best given in the public school. This training in the public schools ought to be carried much further than it usually is. In the city of Newburyport, as I have been informed, there are no exceptions to the custom of educating all the children of the town in the public schools up to the moment when young men enter college. In large towns and cities there is no excuse for the existence of private schools to do the work now done in such schools as those of Newburyport and other places where equal educational privileges exist.

The chief objection brought against the public

school, touching its morality, is derived from the fact that children who are subject to proper moral influences at home are brought in contact with others who are already practised in juvenile vices, if they have not been guilty of petty crimes. I am happy to believe that this statement is not true of many New England communities. The objection was considered in the last Annual Report, — it has been often considered elsewhere; and I do not propose to repeat at length the views which are entertained by the friends of public education.

I have, however, to suggest that while this objection applies with some force to the public school, it applies also to every other school, and that the evil is the least dangerous when the pupil is intrusted to the care of a qualified teacher, who is personally responsible to the public for his conduct, and when the child is also subject to the restraints, and influenced by the daily example and teachings, of the parents.

Moreover, it is to be remembered that the great value of education, in a moral aspect, is the development of the power to resist temptation. This power is not the growth of seclusion; and while neither the teacher nor the parent ought wantonly to expose the child to vicious influences, the school may be even a better preparation for the world from the fact that temptation has there been met, resisted, and overcome. It is also to be remembered that the judgment of parents in a matter so difficult and delicate as a comparison between their own children and other children would not always prove trustworthy nor just; and that a judgment of parties not interested would prove eminently fruitful of dissatisfaction and bitterness.

If all are to be educated, it only remains, then, that they be educated together, subject to the general rule of society, that when a member is dangerous to the safety or peace of his associates, he is to be excluded or restrained. Nor is this necessity of association destitute of moral advantages. If the comparatively good were separated from the relatively vicious, it is not improbable that the latter would soon fall into a state of barbarity. It seems to be the law of the school and of the world that the most rapid progress is made when the weight of public sentiment is on the side of improvement and virtue. It is not necessary for me to remark that such a public sentiment exists in every town and school district of the state; but who would take the responsibility in any of these communities, great or small, of separating the virtuous classes from the dangerous classes? Parents, from the force of their affections, are manifestly incompetent to do this; and those who are not parents are probably equally incompetent. But, if it were honestly accomplished, who would be responsible for the crushing effects of the measure upon those who were thus excluded from the presence and companionship of the comparatively virtuous? These, often the victims of vicious homes, need more than others the influence and example of the good; and it should be among the chief satisfactions of those who are able to train their own children in the ways of virtue, that thereby a healthful influence is exerted upon the less fortunate of their race. There is also in this course a wise selfishness; for, although *children* may be separated from each other, the circumstances of maturer years will often make the virtuous subject to the influence of the vicious. The safety of society, considered individually or collectively, is not in the virtuous training of any part, however large the proportion, but in the virtuous training of all. I cannot deem it wise policy, whether parental or public, that takes the child from the school on account of the immoral associations that are ordinarily found there, or, on the other hand, that drives the vicious or unfortunate from the presence of those who are comparatively pure. When it is considered that the school is often the only refuge of the unhappy subject of orphanage, or the victim of evil family influences, it seems an unnecessary cruelty to withhold the protection, encouragement, and support, which may be so easily and profitably furnished. It is said that a sparrow pursued by a hawk took refuge in the bosom of a member of the sovereign assembly of Athens, and that the harsh Areopagite threw the trembling bird from him with such violence that it was killed on the spot. The assembly was filled with indignation at the cruelty of the deed; the author of it was arraigned as an alien to that sentiment of mercy so necessary to the administration of justice, and by the unanimous suffrages of his colleagues was degraded from the senatorial dignity which he had so much dishonored.

It does not seem necessary to offer an argument in support of the position that the public school is not unfavorably affected, morally, by the fact that it is subject to the popular judgment. This judgment can be rendered only at stated times, and under the forms and solemnities of law. The history of public schools would probably furnish but few instances of wrong in this respect. The people are usually sensitive in regard to the moral character of teachers; they contribute liberally for the support of the schools, are anxious for their improvement, and there is no safer depositary of a trust that is essential to a nation in which is the hope of freedom and free institutions.

And, last, a school cannot be truly said to be destitute of moral character and influence in which the sacred Scriptures are daily read.

The observance of this requirement is a recognition of the existence of the Supreme Being, of the Bible as containing a record of his will concerning men, and of the common duty of rational creatures to live in obedience to the obligations of morality and religion.

It has been no part of my purpose, in this discussion of the public school as an institution fitted to promote morality, to deny the existence of serious defects, or to screen them from the eyes of men. The public school needs a more thorough discipline, a purer morality, a clearer conception and a more practical recognition of the truths of Christianity. But, viewed as a human institution, it claims the general gratitude for the good it has already accomplished. The public school was established in Massachusetts that "learning might not be buried in the graves of our forefathers, in church and commonwealth;" and, in some measure, at least, the early expectation thus quaintly expressed has been realized. Learning has ever been cherished and honored among us. The means of education have been the possession of all; and the enjoyment of these means, often inadequate and humble, has developed a taste for learning, which has been gratified in higher institutions; and thus continually have the resources of the state been magnified, and its influence in the land has been efficient in all that concerns the welfare of the human race on the American continent.

REFORMATION OF CHILDREN.

[Address at the Inauguration of WILLIAM E. STARR, Superintendent of the State Reform School at Westborough.]

NEITHER the invitation of the Trustees nor my own convenience will permit a detailed examination of the topics which the occasion suggests; and it is my purpose to address myself to those who are assembled to participate in the exercises of the day, trusting to familiar and unobserved visits for other and better opportunities for conference with the inmates of the institution.

As the mariner, though cheered by genial winds and canopied by cloudless skies, tests and marks his position and course by repeated observations, so we now desire to note the progress of this humanity-freighted vessel in its voyage over an uncertain sea, yet, as we trust, toward lands of perpetual security and peace. All are voyagers on the sea of life. Some, with the knowledge of ancient days only, grope their way by headlands, or trust themselves occasionally to the guidance of the sun or the stars; while others, with the chart and compass of the

Christian era, move confidently on their course, attracted by the Source and Centre of all good. And it is a blessing of this state of existence, though it may sometimes seem to be a curse, that the choice between good and evil yet remains. The wisdom of a right choice is here manifested in the benevolence of this foundation.

The State Reform School for Boys has now enjoyed eight full years of life and progress; and, though we cannot estimate nor measure the good it may have induced, or the evil it may have prevented, yet enough of its history and results is known to justify the course of its patrons, both public and private, and to warrant the ultimate realization of their early cherished hopes. The state is most honored in the honor awarded to its sons; and the name of LYMAN, now and evermore associated with a work of benevolence and reform, will always command the admiration of the citizens of the commonwealth, and stimulate the youth of the school to acquire and practise those virtues which their generous patron cherished in his own life and honored in others. Governor Washburn, in the Dedication Address, said, "We commend this school, with its officers and inmates, to a generous and grateful public, with the trust that the future lives of the young, who may be sent hither for correction and reform, may prove the crowning glory of an enterprise so auspiciously begun." Since these words were uttered, and this hope, the hope of many hearts, was expressed, nearly two thousand boys, charged with various offences, — many of them petty, and others serious or even criminal, — have been admitted to the school; and the chaplain, in his report for the year 1854, says that "the institution will be instrumental in saving a majority of those who come under its fostering care." This opinion, based, no doubt, upon the experience which the chaplain and other officers of the institution had had, is to be taken as possessing a substantial basis of truth; and it at once suggests important reflections.

Massachusetts is relieved of the presence of a thousand criminal, or, at best, viciously disposed persons. A thousand active, capable, industrious, productive, full-grown men have been created; or, rather, a thousand consumers of the wealth of others, enemies of the public order and peace, have been transformed into intelligent supporters of social life, into generous, faithful guardians of public virtue and tranquillity. Nor would the influences of this degraded population, if unreformed, have ceased with its own existence; every succeeding generation must have gathered somewhat of a harvest of crime and woe. A thousand boys, hardened by neglect, educated in vice, and shunned by the virtuous, would, as men, have been efficient missionaries of lawlessness, wrong, and crime. And who shall estimate how much their reform adds, in its results, to the wealth, the intellectual, moral, and religious character, of the state? The criminal class is never a producing class; and the labor of a thousand men here reclaimed, if estimated for the period of twenty years only, is equal to the labor of twenty thousand men for one year, which, at a hundred dollars each, yields two millions of dollars. The pecuniary advantages of this school, as of all schools, we may estimate; but there are better and higher considerations, in the elevated intellectual, moral, and religious life of the state, that are too pure, too ethereal, to be weighed in the balance against the grosser possessions and acquisitions of society. We thus get glimpses of the prophetic wisdom which led Mr. Lyman to say, "I do not look on this school as an experiment; on the contrary, it strikes me that it is an institution which will produce decidedly beneficial results, not only for the present day, but for many years to come. I do not, therefore, think that it should, even now, be treated in any respect in the light of an experiment, to be abandoned if not successful; for, if the school is introduced to public notice on no better footing and with no more preparation than usually attend trial-schemes of most kinds, the probability is that it will fail, considering the peculiar difficulties of the case." Here is a high order of faith in its application to human affairs; but Mr. Lyman saw, also, that the work to be performed must encounter obstacles, and that its progress toward a perfect result would be slow.

These obstacles have been encountered; and yet the progress has been more rapid than the words of our founder imply. But are we not at liberty to forget the trials, crosses, and perplexities, of this movement, as we behold the fruits, already maturing, of the wisdom and Christian benevolence of our honored commonwealth?

We are assembled to review the past, and to gather from it strength and courage for the future; and we may with propriety congratulate all, whether present or absent, who have been charged with the administration of this school, and have contributed their share, however humble, to promote these benign results. And we ought, also, to remember those, whether living or dead, whose faith and labors laid the foundation on which the state has built. Of the dead, I mention Lyman, Lamb, Denny, Woodward, Shaw, and Greenleaf, — all of whom, with money, counsel, or personal service, contributed to the plan, progress, and completion, of the work.

The good that they have done is not interred with their bones ; and their example will yet find many imitators, as men more generally and more perfectly realize the importance of faith in childhood and youth, as the element of a true faith in our race. If this enterprise, in the judgment of its founder, was not an experiment ten years ago, it cannot be so regarded now ; yet the public will look with anxiety, though with hope, upon every change of the officers of the institution. The trustees having appointed a new superintendent, he now assumes the great responsibility. It may not be second to any in the state ; yet a man of energy, who is influenced by a desire to do good, and who will not measure his reward by present emoluments or temporary fame, can bear steadily and firmly the weight put upon him. The superintendent elect has been a teacher elsewhere, and he is to be a teacher here also. His work will not, in all particulars, correspond with the work that he has left ; yet the principles of government and education are in substance the same. The head of a school always occupies a position of influence ; the characters of the children and youth confided to him are in a great degree subject to his control. Here the teacher is neither aided nor impeded by the usual home influences. This institution is at once a home and a school ; and its head has the united power and responsibility of the parent and the teacher. Here are to be combined the social and moral influences of home, the religious influences of the Sunday-school, with the intellectual and moral training of the public school. He who to-day enters upon this work should have both faith and courage. He is to deal with the unfortunate rather than with the exceptional cases of humanity; for all these are children whom the Father of the race, in his providence, has confided to earthly parents to be educated for a temporal and an immortal existence. That these parents, through crime, ignorance, indolence, carelessness, or misfortune, have failed in their work, is no certain evidence that we are to fail in ours. May we not hope to see in this school the kindness, consideration, affection, and forethought, of the parent, without the delusion which sometimes causes the father or mother to treat the vices of the child as virtues, to be encouraged? And may we not expect from the superintendent, to whom, practically, the discipline of the school is confided, one characteristic of good government, not always, it is feared, found in punitive and reformatory institutions? I speak of the attributes of equality, uniformity, and certainty, in the administration of the law. To be sure, a school, a prison, or a state, will suffer when its code is lax; and it will also suffer when its system is oppressive or sanguinary; but these peculiarities in themselves do not so often, in any community, produce dissatisfaction, disorder, and violence, as an unequal, partial, and uncertain administration of the laws. If at times the laws are administered strictly according to the letter, and if at other times they are reluctantly enforced or altogether disregarded; if it can never be known beforehand whether a violation is to be followed by the prescribed penalty—especially if this uncertainty becomes systematic, and a portion are favored, while the remainder are required to answer strictly for all their delinquencies; and if, above all, these favored ones are recognized as sentinels, or spies, or informers in the service of the officers,—then not only will the spirit of insubordination manifest itself, but that spirit may ripen into alienations, feuds, and personal enmities, dangerous to the prosperity of the institution. Here the scales of justice should be evenly balanced, and the boy should learn, from his own daily experience, to measure equal and exact justice unto others. I do not speak of systems of government: they are essential, no doubt; but they are not to be regarded as of the first importance in institutions for punishment or reformation. Establish as wise a system as you can; but never trust to that alone. Administer the system that you have with all the equality, uniformity, and certainty, that you can command. As a general truth, it may be said that the law is respected when these qualities are exhibited in its administration ; and, when these qualities are wanting, the spirit of obedience is driven from the hearts and minds of the people.

But we are not to rely altogether, nor even chiefly, upon the visible weapons of authority. Especially must the mind and heart of childhood and youth be approached and quickened and strengthened by judicious appeals to the sentiments of veneration and love, and to the principles of the Christian faith. In this institution, one serious obstacle is present; yet it may be overcome by energy, industry, and a spirit of benevolence. I speak of the large number of inmates to be superintended by one person. Men act in masses for the removal of general evils ; but the reformation of children must be individual, and to a great extent dependent upon the agency, or at least upon the coöperation, of the subjects of it. It is not easy for the superintendent to make himself acquainted with the persons and familiar with the lives of six hundred boys ; yet this knowledge is quite essential to the exercise of a salutary influence over them. He may be aided by the subordinate officers of the institution ; and that aid, under any circumstances, he will need: but, after all, his own influence and power for good will be measured by the extent of his personal acquaintance with the inmates as individuals. First, then, government is essential to this school; not a reign of terror, but a government whose majesty, power, equality, certainty, uniformity, and consequent justice, shall be experienced by all alike; and, being experienced by all alike, will be respected, reverenced, and obeyed.

And next the social, intellectual, and moral influences of the school and the home should be combined and mingled, or else the visible forms of government become a skeleton, merely indicating the figure, structure, and outline, of the perfect body, but destitute of the vital principle which alone could render it of any value to itself or to the world.

This institution is not an end, but a means. The home itself is only a preparatory school for life. This is a substitute for the home, but is not, and never can be, its equal. It therefore follows that a boy should be removed whenever a home can be secured, especially if his reformation has been previously so far accomplished as to render the completion of the work probable.

A great trust has been confided to the officers of the Reform School; but the power to do good is usually proportionate to the responsibility imposed upon the laborer. In this view, much will be expected; but the expectations formed ought not to relate so much to results as to the wisdom and humanity with which the operations are conducted. Massachusetts is charged with the support of a great number of charitable and reformatory institutions. Their necessity springs from the defects of social life; therefore their existence is a comparative rather than a positive good; and he is the truest friend of the race who does most to remove the causes of poverty, ignorance, insanity, mental and physical weakness, moral waywardness, and crime.

THE CARE AND REFORMATION OF THE NEGLECTED AND EXPOSED CLASSES OF CHILDREN.

[An Address delivered at the opening of the State Industrial School for Girls, at Lancaster, Massachusetts.]

In man's limited view, the moral world presents a sad contrast to the natural. The natural world is harmonious in all its parts; but the moral world is the theatre of disturbing and conflicting forces, whose laws the finite mind cannot comprehend. The majesty and uniformity of the planetary revolutions, which bring day and night, summer and winter, seed-time and harvest, know no change. Worlds and systems of worlds are guided by a law of the Infinite Mind; and so, through unnumbered years and myriads of years, birth and death, creation and decay, decrees whose fixedness enables finite minds to predict the future, and rules whose elasticity is seen in a never-ending variety of nature, all alike prove that the sin of disobedience is upon man alone.

But, if man only, of all the varied creations of earth, may fall from his high estate, so to him only is given the power to rise again, and feebly, yet with faith, advance towards the Divine Excellence. This, then, is the great thought of the occasion, to be accepted by the hearts and illustrated in the lives of all. The fallen may be raised up, the exposed may be shielded, the wanderers may be called home, or else this house is built upon the sand, and doomed to fall when the rains shall descend, the floods come, and the winds blow. The returning autumn, with its harvest of sustenance and wealth, bids us contemplate again the mystery and harmony of the natural world. The tree and the herb produce seed, and the seed again produces the tree and the herb, each after its kind. There is a continued production and reproduction; but of responsibility there is none. As there is no intelligent violation of law, there is no accountability. Man, however, is an intelligent, dependent, fallible, and, of course, responsible being. He is responsible for himself, responsible in some degree for his fellow-man. There is not a chapter in the history of the human race, nor a day of its experience, which does not show that the individual members are dependent upon, and responsible to, each other. This great fact, of six thousand years' duration, at once presents to us the necessity for government, and defines the limits of its powers and duties. Government, then, is a union of all for the protection and welfare of each. This definition presents, in its principles and statement, the highest form of human government, — a form not yet perfectly realized on earth. It sets forth rather what government ought to be, than what it has been or is. Too often historical governments, and living governments even, may be defined as a union of a few for their benefit, and for the oppression of many. The reason of man has not often been consulted in their formation, and the interests and principles of the masses have usually been disregarded in their administration.

A true government is at once representative, patriarchal, and paternal. In the path of duty for this day and this occasion, we shall consider the last-named quality only, — governments should be paternal. The paternal government is devoted to the elevation and improvement of its members, with no ulterior motive except the necessary results of internal purity and strength. Every government is, in some degree, no doubt, paternal. Nor are those governments to be regarded as eminently so, where the people are most controlled in their private, personal affairs. These are mere despotisms ; and despotism is not a just nor necessary element of the paternal relation. That government is most truly paternal which does most to enable its citizens or subjects to regulate their own conduct, and determine their relations to others. In the midst of general darkness, the paternal element of government has been a light to the human race. It modified the patriarchal slavery of the Hebrews, relieved the iron rule of Sparta, made European feudalism the hope of civilization in the Dark Ages, and the basis of its coming glories in the near future ; and it now leads men to look with toleration upon the despotism of Russia, and with kindness upon the simplicity and arrogance of the Celestial Empire.

We complain, justly enough, that the world is governed too much ; and yet, in a great degree, we neglect the means by which the proper relations of society could be preserved, and the world be governed less. In what works are the so-called Christian governments principally engaged ? Are they not seeking, by artifice, diplomacy, and war, to extend national boundaries, preserve national honor, or enforce nice distinctions against the timid and weak ? Yet it is plain that a nation is powerful according to the character of the living elements of which it is composed. If it is disorganized morally, uncultivated in intellect, ignorant, indolent, or wasteful in its labor, its claims to greatness are destitute of solid foundation, and it must finally yield to those that have sought and gained power by the elevation of the individual as the element of the nation.

That nation, then, is wise, and destined to become truly great, which cultivates the best elements of individual life and character. It is not enough to read the parable of the lost sheep, and of the ninety and nine that went not astray, and then say, "Even so, it is not the will of your Father which is in heaven that one of these little ones should perish," while the means of salvation, as regards the life of this world merely, are very generally neglected. Such neglect is followed by error and crime; and error and crime are followed by judgment not always tempered with mercy.

While human governments debate questions of war and peace, of trade and revenue, of annexations with ceremony, and appropriations of territory without ceremony, who shall answer to the Governor and Judge of all for the neglect, indifference, and oppression, which beget and foster the delinquencies of childhood, and harden the criminals of adult life?

And who shall answer for those distinctions of caste and systems of labor which so degrade and famish masses of human beings, that the divine miracle of the feeding of the five thousand must be multiplied many times over before the truths of nature or revelation can be received into teachable minds or susceptible hearts? And who shall answer for the hereditary poverty, ignorance and crime, which constitute a marked feature of English life, and are distinctly visible upon the face of American civilization? These questions may point with sufficient distinctness to the sources of the evils enumerated; but we are not to assume that mere human governments can furnish an adequate and complete remedy. Yet this admitted inability to do everything is no excuse for neglecting those things which are plainly within their power. Taking upon themselves the parental character, forgetting that they have wrongs to avenge, and seeking reformation through kindness, criminals and the causes of crime will diminish, if they do not disappear. This is the responsibility of the nations, and the claim now made upon them. Individual civilization and refinement have always been in advance of national; and national character is the mirrored image of the individual characters, not excepting the humblest, of which the nation is composed. Each foot of the ocean's surface has, in its fluidity or density or position, something of the quality or power of every drop of water which rests or moves in the depths of the sea. What is called national character is the face of the great society beneath; and, as that society in its elements is elevated or debased, so will the national character rise or fall in the estimation of all just men, and upon the page of impartial history. Government, which is the organized expression of the will of society, should represent the best elements of which society is composed; and it ought, therefore, to combat error and wrong, and seek to inaugurate labor, justice, and truth, as the elements of stability, growth, and power. It must accept as its principles of action the best rules of conduct in individuals. The man who avenges his personal wrongs by personal attacks or vindictive retaliation, must sacrifice in some measure the sympathy of the wise, the humane, and the good. So the nation which avenges real or fancied wrongs crushes out the elements of humanity and a higher life, which, properly cultivated, might lead an erring mortal to virtue and peace. The proper object of punishment is not vengeance, but the public safety and the reformation of the criminal. Indeed, we may say that the sole object of punishment is the reformation of the criminal; for there can be no safety to the public while the criminal is unreformed. The punishment of the prison must, from its nature, be temporary; perpetual confinement can be meted out to a few great crimes only. If, then, the result of punishment be vengeance, and not reformation, the last state of society is worse than its first. The prison must stand a sad monument of the want of true paternal government in the family and the state; but, when it becomes the receptacle merely of the criminal, and all ideas of reformation are banished from the hearts of convicts and the minds of keepers, its influence is evil, and only evil continually.

Vice, driven from the presence of virtue, with no hope of reformation or of restoration to society, begets vice, and becomes daily more and more loathsome. Misery is so universal that some share falls to the lot of all; but that misery whose depths cannot be sounded, whose heights cannot be scaled, is the fortune of the prison convict only, who has no hope of reformation to virtue or of restoration to the world. His is the only misery that is unrelieved; his is the only burden that is too great to be borne. To him the foliage of the tree, the murmur of the brook, the mirror of the quiet lake, or the thunder of the heaving ocean, would be equally acceptable. His separation from nature is no less burdensome than his separation from man. The heart sinks, the spirit turns with a consuming fire upon itself, the soul is in despair; the mind is first nerved and desperate, then wandering and savage, then idiotic, and finally goes out in death. Governments cannot often afford to protect themselves, or to avenge themselves, at such a cost. There may be great crimes on which such awful penalties should be visited; but, for the honor of the race, let them be few.

We may err in our ideas of the true relations of the prison to the prisoner. We call a prison good or bad when we see its walls, cells, workshops, its means of security, and points of observation. These are very well. They are something; but they are not all. We might so judge a hospital for the sick; and we did once so judge an asylum for the insane.

But what to the sick man are walls of wood, brick, granite, or marble? What are towers and turrets, what are wards, halls, and verandas, if withal he is not cheered and sustained by the sympathizing heart and helping hand? And similar preparations furnish for the insane personal security and physical comfort; but can they

> "Minister to a mind diseased;
> Pluck from the memory a rooted sorrow;
> Raze out the written troubles of the brain?"

And it may be that the old almshouse at Philadelphia, which was nearly destitute of material aids, and had only superintendent, matrons, and assistants, was, all in all, the best insane asylum in America.

We cannot neglect the claims of security, discipline, and labor, in the erection of jails and prisons; but to acknowledge these merely will never produce the proper fruit of punishment — reformation. Indeed, walls of stone, gates of iron, bolts, locks, and armed sentinels, though essential to security, without which there could be neither punishment nor reformation, are in themselves barriers rather than helps to moral progress. Standing outside, we cannot say what should be done either in the insane hospital or the prison; but we can deduce from the experience of modern times a safe rule for general conduct. In the insane hospital the patient is to be treated as though he were sane; and in the jail the prisoner is to be treated, nearly as may be, as though he were virtuous. This rule, especially as much of it as applies to the prisoner, may be recklessness to some, to others folly, to others sin.

"The court awards it, and the law doth give it," is no doubt the essence and strength of governmental justice in the sentence decreed; but it would be a sad calamity if there were no escape from its literal fulfilment. And let no one borrow the words of Portia to the Jew, and say to the state,

> "Nor cut thou less nor more,
> But just a pound of flesh."

As the criminal staggers beneath the accumulated weight of his sin and its penalty, he should feel that the state is not only just in the language of its law, but merciful in its administration; that the government is, in truth, paternal. This feeling inspires confidence and hope; and without these there can be no reformation. And, following this thought, we are led to say, it is a sad and mischievous public delusion that the pardoning power is useless or pernicious. It is a *delusion;* for it is the only means by which the state mingles mercy with its justice,—the means by which the better sentiments of the prison are marshalled in favor of order, of law, of progress. It is a *public delusion;* for it has infected not only the masses of society, who know little of what is going on in courts and prisons, but its influence is observed upon the bench and in the bar, especially among those who are accustomed to prosecute and try criminals. This is not strange, nor shall it be a subject of complaint; but we must not always look upon the prisoner as a criminal, and continually disregard his claims as a man. It is not often easy, nor always possible, to make the proper distinction between the *character* and *condition* of the prisoner. But the prison, strange as it may seem, follows the general law of life. It has its public sentiment, its classes, its leading minds, as well as the university or the state; it has its men of mark, either good or bad, as well as congress or parliament. As the family, the church, or the school, is the reflection of the best face of society, so the prison is the reflection of the worst face of society. But it nevertheless is society, and follows its laws with as much fidelity as the world at large.

It is said that Abbé Fissiaux, the head of the colony of Marseilles, when visiting Mettray, a kind of reform school, at which boys under sixteen years of age, who have committed offences without discernment, are sent, asked the colonists to point out to him the three best boys. The looks of the whole body immediately designated three young persons whose conduct had been irreproachable to an exceptional degree. He then applied a more delicate test. "Point out to me," said he, "the worst boy." All the children remained motionless, and made no sign; but one little urchin came forward, with a pitiful air, and said, in a very low tone, "*It is me.*" Such were the public sentiment and sense of honor, even in a reform school. This frankness in the lad was followed by reformation; and he became in after years a good soldier, — the life anticipated for many members of the institution.

The pardoning power is not needed in reform and industrial schools, where the managers have discretionary authority; but it is quite essential to the discipline of the prison to let the light of hope into the prisoner's heart. Not that all are to enjoy the benefits of executive clemency, — by no means: only the most worthy and promising are to be thus favored. But, for many years, the Massachusetts prison has been improved and elevated in its tone and sentiment above what it would have been; while, as it is believed, over ninety per cent. of the convicts thus discharged have conducted themselves well. If the prisoner's conduct has not been, upon the whole, reasonably good, and for a long time irreproachable, he has no chance for clemency; and, whatever may be his conduct, and whatever may be the hopes inspired, he should not be allowed to pass without the prison walls until a friend, labor, and a home, are secured for him. And the exercise of the pardoning power, if it anticipate the expiration of the legal sentence but a month, a week, or a day even, may change the whole subsequent life. Men, criminals, convicts, are not insensible to kindness; and when the government shortens the legal sentence, which is usually their measure of justice, they feel an additional obligation to so behave as to bring no discredit upon a power which has been a source of inestimable joy to them. And prisoners thus discharged have often gone forth with a feeling that the hopes of many whom they had left behind were centred in them.

Mr. Charles Forster, of Charlestown, says, in a letter to me: "I have been connected with the Massachusetts State Prison for a period of thirty-eight years, and have always felt a strong interest in the improvement, welfare, and happiness, of the unfortunate men confined within its walls. I am conversant with many touching cases of deep and heartfelt gratitude for kindly acts and sympathy bestowed upon them, both during and subsequent to their imprisonment." And the same gentleman says further, "I think that the proportion of persons discharged from prison by executive clemency, who have subsequently been convicted of penal offences, is very small indeed." To some, whose imaginations have pictured a broad waste or deep gulf between themselves and the prisoner class, these may seem strange words; but there is no mystery in this language to those who have listened to individual cases of crime and punishment. Men are tried and convicted of crimes according to rules and definitions which are necessarily arbitrary and technical; but the moral character of criminals is not very well defined by the rules and definitions which have been applied to their respective cases. Our prisons contain men who are great and professional criminals, — men who advisedly follow a life of crime themselves, and deliberately educate generation after generation to a career of infamy and vice. As a general thing, mercy to such men would be unpardonable folly. Of them I do not now speak. But there is another class, who are involved in guilt and its punishment through the defects of early education, the misfortune of orphanage, accident, sudden temptation, or the influence of evil companionship in youth.

The field from which this class is gathered is an extensive one, and its outer limits are near to every hearthstone. To all these, prison life, unless it is relieved by a hope of restoration to the world at the hand of mercy, is the school of vice, and a certain preparation for a career of crime. As a matter of fact, this class does furnish recruits to supply the places of the hardened villains who annually die, or permanently forsake the abodes of civilized men. What hope can there be for a young man who remains in prison until the last day of his sentence is measured by the sun in his course, and then passes into the world, with the mark of disgrace and the mantle of shame upon him, to the society of the companions by whose influence he first fell? For such a one there can be no hope. And be it always remembered that there are those without the prison walls, as well as many within, who resist every effort to bring the wanderers back to obedience and right. I was present at the prison in Charlestown when the model of a bank-lock was taken from a young man whose term had nearly expired. The model was cut in wood, after a plan drawn upon sand-paper by an experienced criminal, then recently convicted. This old offender was so familiar with the lock, that he was able to reproduce all its parts from memory alone. This fact shows the influence that may be exerted, even in prison, upon the characters of the young and less vicious. Now, can any doubt that these classes, as classes, ought to be separated? Nor let the question be met by the old statement, that all communication between prisoners should be cut off. Humanity cannot defend, as a permanent system, the plan which shuts up the criminal, unless he is a murderer, from the light of the human countenance. Such penalties foster crimes, whose roots take hold of the state itself.

The result of the exercise of the pardoning power is believed to have been, upon the whole, satisfactory. This is the concurrent testimony of officers and others whose opinions are entitled to weight. Permit the statement of a single case, to which many similar ones might be added. In a remote state of the West there is a respectable and successful farmer, who was once sentenced to the penitentiary for life. His crime was committed in a moment of desperation, produced by the contrast

9*

between a state of abject poverty in a strange land, at the age of twenty-three, and the recollection of childhood and youth passed beneath the parental roof, surrounded by the comforts and conveniences of the well-educated and well-conditioned classes of English society. This, it is true, was a peculiar case. It was marked in the circumstances and enormity of the crime, and marked in the subsequent good conduct of the prisoner. But can any one object, that, after ten years' imprisonment, this man was allowed to try his fortunes once more among his fellow-men? Are there those who would have had no faith in his uninterrupted good conduct; in the abundant evidence of complete reformation; in the fact that, in prison and poverty and disgrace, he had allied to him friends of name and fortune and Christian virtues, who were ready to aid him in his good resolutions? If any such there be, let them visit the solitary cell of the despairing convict, whose crime is so great that executive clemency fears to approach it. Crime and despair have made the features appalling; all the worst passions of our nature riot together in the temple made for the living God; and the death of the body is almost certainly to be preceded by madness, insanity, and idiocy of the mind. Or, if any think that this person escaped with too light an expiation for so great a crime, let them recall the incident of the youth who was questioned because he looked with fond affection into the babbling face of the running brook, and, apologizing, as it were, in reply said, "O, yes, it is very beautiful, and especially to me, who have seen no water for four years, beside what I have had to drink!"

Nor is it assumed, in all that is said upon this subject, that the laws are severe, or that the judicial administration of them is not characterized by justice and mercy. In the ordinary course of affairs, the pardoning power is not resorted to for the correction of any error or injustice of the courts; but it is the means by which the state tempers its justice with mercy; and, if the penalties for crime were less than they are, the necessity for the exercise of this power would still remain. It assumes that the object of the penal law is reformation; and if this object, in some cases, can be attained by the exercise of the pardoning power, while the rigid execution of the sentence would leave the criminal, as it usually will, still hardened and unrepenting, is it not wise for the state to benefit itself, and save the prisoner, by opening the prison-doors, and inviting the convict to a life of industry and virtue? And let it never be forgotten, though it is the lowest view which can be taken of crime and prisons, that the criminal class is the most expensive class of society. In general, it is a non-producing class, and, whether in prison or out, is a heavy burden upon the public. The mere interest of the money now expended in prisons of approved structure is, for each cell, equal annually to the net income of a laboring man ; and professional thieves, when at large, often gather by their art, and expend in profligacy, many thousand dollars a year. And here we see how much wiser it is, in an economical point of view, to save the child, or reform the man, than to allow the adult criminal to go at large, or provide for his safe-keeping at the expense of the state.

Under the influence of the pardoning power, wisely executed, the commonwealth becomes a family, whose law is the law of kindness. It is the paternal element of government applied to a class of people who, by every process of reasoning, would be found least susceptible to its influence. It is the great power of the state, both in the wisdom required for its judicious exercise, and in the beneficial results to which it may lead. Men may desire office for its emoluments in money or fame; they may seek it in a spirit of rivalry, or for personal pride, or for the opportunity it brings to reward friends and punish enemies ; but all these are poor and paltry compared with the divine privilege, exercised always in reference to the public welfare, of elevating the prisoner to the companionship of men, and cheering him with words of encouragement on his entrance anew to the duties of life.

Yet think not that the prison is a reformatory institution : far from it. If the prison should be left to the influence of legitimate prison discipline merely, it is doubtful whether the sum of improvement would equal the total of degradation. This may be said of the best prisons of America, of New England. The prison usually contains every class, from the hardened convict, incarcerated for house-breaking, robbery, or murder, to the youth who expiates his first offence, committed under the influence of evil companions, or sudden temptation. The contact of these two persons must be injurious to one of them, without in any degree improving the other. Therefore the prison, considered without reference to the elevating influence of the pardoning power, has but little ability to reform the bad, and yet possesses a sad tendency to debase the comparatively good.

We miss, too, in the prison, another essential element of a reformatory institution. Reformation in individual cases may take place under the most adverse circumstances ; but an institution cannot be called reformatory unless its prevailing moral sentiment is actively, vigorously, and always, on the side of progress and virtue. This moral influence must proceed from the officers of the institution ; but it should be increased and strengthened by the sympathy and support of the inmates. This can hardly be expected of the prison. The number of adult persons experienced in crime and hardened by its penalties is usually so large, that the moral sentiment of the officers, and the weak resolutions of the small class of prisoners, who, under favorable circumstances, might be saved, are insufficient to give a healthy tone to the whole institution. The prison is a battle-field of vice and virtue, with the advantage of position and numbers on the side of vice. Indeed, there can hardly be a worse place for the young or the inexperienced in crime. This is the testimony of reason and of all experience ; yet the public mind is slow to accept the remedy for the evil. It is a privilege to believe that the worst scenes of prison life are not found in the United States. Consider this case, reported in an English journal, *The Ragged-School Magazine* :

"D. F., aged about fourteen. Mother dead several years ; father a drunkard, and deserted him about three years ago. Has since lived as he best could, — sometimes going errands, sometimes begging and thieving. Slept in lodging-houses when he had money ; but very often walked the streets at night, or lay under arches or door-steps. Has only one brother ; he lives by thieving. Does not know where he is ; has no other friend that he knows ; never learnt to read ; was badly off ; picked a handkerchief out of a gentleman's pocket, and was caught by a policeman ; sent to Giltspur-street Prison ; was fed on bread and water ; instructed every day by chaplain and schoolmaster ; much impressed with what the chaplain said ; felt anxious to do better ; behaved well in prison ; *was well flogged the morning he left ; back bruised, but not quite bleeding ;* was then turned into the street, ragged, barefooted, friendless, homeless, penniless ; walked about the streets till afternoon, when he received a penny from a gentleman to buy a loaf ; met, next day, some expert thieves in the Minories ; went along with them, and continues in a course of vagrancy and crime."

And what else could have been expected ? The government, having sown tares, had no right to gather wheat. Yet, had this boy been provided with a home, either in a family or a reform school, with sufficient labor, and proper moral and intellectual culture, he might have been saved. Of the three thousand persons annually in prison at Newgate, four hundred are less than sixteen years of age ; and twenty thousand children and youth under seventeen years of age yearly pass through the prisons of England. "Many of the juvenile prisoners," it is said, "have been frequently in prison, and are very hardened. Some, from nine to eleven, have been in prison repeatedly, and have very little fear of it."

The officers of the Liverpool Borough Jail are united in the opinion that, when a boy comes once, he is almost certain to come again and again, until he is transported. And, of every one hundred young persons discharged from the principal prisons of Paris, seventy-five are in the custody of the law within the next three months. A professed thief said to the Rev. Mr. Clay, of England, "I am convinced of this, having too bitterly experienced it, that communication in a prison has brought thousands to ruin. I speak not of boys only, but of men and women also." And Mr. Hill, Recorder of Birmingham, says of the sentences imposed in his court, "We are compelled to carry into operation an ignorant and vengeful system, which augments to a fearful extent the very evils it was framed to correct." A few years ago, there was a lad in a New England prison whose experience is a pertinent illustration of the evil we are now considering. His father, a resident of a city, died while the boy was in infancy. He, however, soon passed beyond the control of his mother, and at an early age was selected by a brace of thieves, who petted, caressed, and humored him, until he was completely subject to their will. He was then made useful to them in their profession; but at last they were all arrested while engaged in robbing a store, — the boy being within the building, and the men stationed as sentinels without. In this case, the discretion of the court, which distinguished in the sentence between the hardened villains and the youth, was inadequate to the emergency. The child, unfit for the prison, and sure to be contaminated by it, ought to have been sent to a house of reformation, a reform school, or, perhaps better than either, to the custody of a well-regulated, industrious family. Now, in such cases, the distinction which the law, judicially administered, does not make, and cannot make, must be made by the executive in the wise exercise of the pardoning power. But this power, in the nature of things, has its limits; and on one side it is limited to those who have been convicted of crime.

At this point, we may see how faulty, and yet how constantly improving, has been the administration of the criminal law. First, we have the prison without the pardoning power, except in cases of mal-administration of the law, — a receptacle of the bad and good, where the former are not improved, and the latter are hurried rapidly on in the path of degradation and crime. Then we have the prison under the influence of the pardoning power, more or less wisely administered, but, in its best form, able only to arrest and counteract partially the tendencies to evil. Next, from the imperfections of this system an advancing civilization has evoked the Reform School, which gathers in the young criminals and viciously inclined youth, and prepares them, by labor, and culture of the mind and heart, to resist the temptations of life. But this institution seems to wait, though it may not always in reality do so, until the candidate is actually a criminal.

Hence the necessity which calls us to-day to consider the means adopted elsewhere, and the means now to be employed here, to save the young and exposed from the dangers which surround them.

Passing, then, in review, ladies and gentlemen, the thoughts which have been presented, I deduce from them for your assent and support, if so it please you, the following propositions as the basis of what I have yet to say :

I. Government, in the prevention and punishment of crime, should be paternal.

II. The object of punishment should be reformation, and not revenge.

III. The law of reformation in the state, as in the family, is the law of kindness.

IV. As criminals vary in age and in experience as criminals, so should their treatment vary.

V. Prisons and jails are not, in their foundation and management, reformatory institutions, and only become so through influences not necessarily nor ordinarily acting upon them.

VI. As prisons and jails deter from crime through fear only, exert very little moral influence upon the youth of either sex, and fail in many respects and in a majority of cases as reformatory institutions, we ought to avail ourselves of any new agency which promises success.

Influenced, as we may reasonably suppose, by these or kindred sentiments, and aided by the noblest exhibitions of private benevolence, the state has here founded a school for the prevention of crime. As we have everywhere among us schools whose *leading* object is the development of the intellect, so we now dedicate a school whose *leading* object is the development of the affections as the basis of the cardinal virtues of life.

The design of this institution is so well expressed

by the trustees, that it is a favor to us all for me to read the first chapter of the by-laws, which, by the consent of the Governor and Council, have been established :

"The intention of the state government, and of the benevolent individuals who have contributed to the establishment of this institution, is to secure a *home* and a *school* for such girls as may be presented to the magistrates of the state, appointed for that purpose, as vagrants, perversely obstinate, deprived of the control and culture of their natural guardians, or guilty of petty offences, and exposed to a life of crime and wretchedness.

"For such young persons it is proposed to provide, not a prison for their restraint and correction, but a family school, where, under the firm but kind discipline of a judicious home, they shall be carefully instructed in all the branches of a good education ; their moral affections be developed and cultivated by the example and affectionate care of one who shall hold the relation of a mother to them ; be instructed in useful and appropriate forms of female industry ; and, in short, be fitted to become virtuous and happy members of society, and to take respectable positions in such relations in life as Providence shall hereafter mark out for them.

"It is to be distinctly understood that the institution is not to be considered a *place of punishment*, or its subjects as criminals. It is to be an inviting refuge, into which the exposed may be gathered to be saved from a course which would inevitably end in penal confinement, irretrievable ruin, or hopeless degradation.

"The inmates are to be considered hopeful and promising subjects of appropriate culture, and to be instructed and watched over with the care and kindness which their peculiar exposures demand, and with the confidence which youth should ever inspire.

"The restraint and the discipline which will be necessary are to be such as would be appropriate in a Christian family or in a small boarding-school; and the 'law of kindness' should be written upon the heart of every officer of the institution. The chief end to be obtained, in all the culture and discipline, is the proper development of the faculties and moral affections of the inmates, however they may have been heretofore neglected or perverted; and to teach them the art, and aid them in securing the power, of self-government."

Under the influence of these sentiments, we pass, if possible, in the work of reformation, from the rigor of the prison to the innocent excitement and rivalry of the school, the comfort, confidence and joys of home. This institution assumes that crime, to some extent at least, is social, local, or hereditary, in its origin ; that the career of hardened criminals often takes its rise in poverty, idleness, ignorance, orphanage, desertion, or intemperance of parents, evil example, or the indifference, scorn and neglect of society. It assumes, also, that there is a period of life — childhood and youth — when these, the first indications of moral death, may be eradicated, or their influence for evil controlled. In this land of education, of liberty, of law, of labor and religion, we may not easily imagine how universal the enumerated evils are in many portions of Europe. The existence of these evils is in some degree owing to institutions which favor a few, and oppress the masses ; but it is also in a measure due to the fact that Europe is both old and multitudinous. America, though still young, is even now multitudinous. Hence, both here and there, crime is social and local. The truth of this statement is proportionate to the force of the causes in the respective countries.

We are assembled upon a sloping hillside, overlooking a quiet country village. Happy homes are embowered in living groves, whose summer foliage is emblematical of innocence, progress, and peace. We have here a social life, with natural impulses, cultivated worldly interests, moral and religious sentiments, all on the side of virtue. Crime here is not social. If it appear at all, it is segregated ; and, as the burning taper expires when placed at the centre of the spirit lamp's coiling sheet of flame, so vice and crime cannot thrive in the genial embrace of virtue.

Circumstances are here unfavorable to crime ; it is never social ; but sometimes, though not often, it is hereditary. A family for many generations seems to have a criminal tendency. Perhaps the members are not in any generation guilty of great crimes, but often of lesser ones ; and are, moreover, in the daily practice of vices that give rise to suspicion, neglect, and reproach. Here together are associated, and made hereditary, poverty, ignorance, idleness, beggary, and vagrancy. Surely these instances are not common, probably not so common as they were in the last generation. But how is the boy or girl of such a family to rise above these circumstances, and throw off these weights ? Occasionally one of great energy of character may do so ; but, if the children of more fortunate classes can scarcely escape the influence of temporary evil example, how shall they who are born to a heritage of poverty, ignorance, and ever-present evil counsel and conduct under the guise of parental authority, pass to the position of intelligent, industrious, respectable members of society ? Some external influence must be applied ;

by some means from without, the spell must be broken; the fatal succession of vicious homes must be interrupted. The family has here failed to discharge its duty to itself and to the state; and shall not the state do its duty to itself, by assuming the paternal relation under the guidance of that law of kindness, which we have seen effectual to control the insane, and melt the hardened criminal? But in cities we find vice, not only hereditary in families, but local and social; so that streets and squares are given up, as it were, to the idle and vicious, whose numbers and influence produce and perpetuate a public sentiment in support of their daily practices. This phase of life is not due to the fact that cities are wealthy, or that they are engaged in manufactures or commerce; but to the single fact that they are multitudinous, and their inhabitants are, therefore, in daily contact with each other, while, in the country, individuals and families are comparatively isolated. Yet some may very well doubt whether such an institution as this, with all the benign influences of home which we hope to see centred and diffusive here, will save a child of either sex, whose first years shall have been so unfavorable to a life of virtue.

The answer is plain: as in other reformatory institutions, there will be some successes and some failures. The failures will be reckoned as they were; the successes will be a clear gain.

But investigation and trial will show a natural aptitude or instinct in children that will aid in their improvement and reformation. There has been in one of our public schools a lad, who, at the age of fourteen years, could not recall distinctly the circumstances of his life previous to the time when he was a newsboy in the city of New York. He was ignorant of father, mother, kindred, family name, and nation. At an early age, he travelled through the middle, southern and south-western states, engaged in selling papers and trash literature; and, for a time, he was employed by a showman to stand outside the tent and describe and exaggerate the attractions within. When he was in his fourteenth year, he accepted the offer of a permanent home; his chief object being, as he said, to obtain an education. "I have found," said he, "that a man cannot do much in this country unless he has some learning." This truth, simple, and resting upon a low view of education, may yet be of infinite value if accepted by those who, even among us, are advancing to adult life without the preparation which our common schools are well fitted to furnish. And the case of this lad may be yet further useful by showing how compensation is provided for evils and neglects in mental and moral relations, as well as in the physical and natural world. Though ignorant of books, he was thoroughly and extensively acquainted with things, and consequently made rapid progress in the knowledge of signs ; for they were immediately applied, and of course remembered. In a few months, he took a respectable position among lads of his age. The world had done for this boy what good schools do not always accomplish,— made him familiar with things before he was troubled with the signs which stand for them. There is an ignorance in manhood ; an ignorance under the show of profound learning ; an ignorance for which schools, academies and colleges, are often responsible ; an ignorance that neither schools, academies nor colleges, can conceal from the humblest intellects ; an ignorance of life and things as they are within the sphere of our own observation. From this most deplorable ignorance this boy had escaped ; and the light of learning illumined his mind, as the sun in his daily return reveals anew those forms of life, which, even in an ungenial spring and early summer, his rays had warmed into existence, and nourished and cherished in their progress towards perfection.

And, ladies and gentlemen, let us indulge the hope that the events of this day and the faith of this assembly will declare that it is possible to save the children of orphanage, intemperance, neglect, scorn and ignorance, from many of the evils which surround them. Let it not be assumed and believed that the task of training and saving girls is less hopeful than similar labors in behalf of the other sex. It has been found true in Europe, and it is a prevailing opinion in this country, that, among adults, the reformation of females is more difficult than the reformation of males. But an analysis of this fact, assuming it to be true, will unfold qualities of female character that render it peculiarly easy to shield and save girls who are exposed to a life of crime; for, be it remembered, this institution deals with mere children, who are exposed, but not yet lost. It differs, in this respect, from most institutions, although many include this class with others. And it may be well to remark, that every reformatory school in Europe, even those altogether penal, — as Parkhurst in England, and Mettray in France, — have had some measure of success. Eighty-nine per cent. of the colons, or convicts, at Mettray, have become respectable and useful; while, of the youth sent to the ordinary jails and prisons, seventy-five per cent. are totally lost. It is not fair, therefore, to assume that this attempt will fail. The degree of success will depend upon circumstances and causes, to a great extent, within human control. There are, however, three elements of success, so distinct that they may well stand as the appropriate divisions of what remains for consideration. They are the right action of the government; the faithful conduct of superintendent, matrons, and assistants; the sympathy and aid of the people of the state in matters which do not admit of legislative interference.

The act of the Legislature, though voluminous in its details, contemplates only this: A home for girls between seven and sixteen years of age, who are found "in circumstances of want and suffering, or of neglect, exposure, or abandonment, or of beggary." The first idea of *home* precludes the possibility of the inmates being sent here as a punishment for crime; therefore they are neither adjudged nor actual criminals, but persons exposed to a vicious life. Secondly, the idea of home involves the necessity of reproducing the family relation, as circumstances may permit. Hence, the members of this institution are to be divided into families; and over each a matron will preside, who is to be a kind, affectionate, discreet mother to the children.

And here, for once, in Massachusetts, a public institution has escaped the tyranny of bricks and mortar; and we are permitted to indulge the hope, that any future additions will tend to make this spot a neighborhood of unostentatious cottages, quiet rural homes, rather than the seat of a vast edifice, which may provoke the wonder of the sight-seer, inflame local or state pride, but can never be an effectual, economical agency in the work of reformation. Every public institution has some great object. Architecture should bend itself to that object, and become its servant; and it must ever be deemed a mistake, when utility is sacrificed that art or fancy may have its way.

Reformation, if wrought by external influences, is the result of personal kindness. Personal kindness can exist only where there is intimate personal acquaintance; this acquaintance is impossible in an institution of two, three, or five hundred inmates. But, in a family of ten, twenty, or thirty, this knowledge will exist, and this kindness abound. Warm personal attachments will grow up in the family, and these attachments are likely to become safeguards of virtue.

Nor let the objection prevail that the expense is to be increased. It is not the purpose to set up an establishment and maintain it for a specific sum of money, but to provide thorough mental and moral training for the inmates. Make the work efficient, though it be limited to a small number, rather than inaugurate a magnificent failure.

The state has wisely provided that the "trustees shall cause the girls under their charge to be instructed in piety and morality, and in such branches of useful knowledge as shall be adapted to their age and capacity; they shall also be instructed in some regular course of labor, either mechanical, manufacturing, or horticultural, or a combination of these, and especially in such domestic and household labor and duties as shall be best suited to their age and strength, disposition and capacity; also in such other arts, trades, and employments, as may seem to the trustees best adapted to secure their reformation, amendment, and future benefit."

It is sometimes the bane of the poor that they do not work, and it is often equally the bane of the rich that they have nothing to do. The idle, both rich and poor, carry a weight of reproach that not all ought to bear. The disposition and the ability to labor are both the result of education; and why should the uneducated be better able to labor than to read Greek and Latin? Surely only that there are more teachers in one department than in the others; but a good teacher of labor may be as uncommon as a good teacher of Latin or Greek. There is a false, vicious, unmanly pride, which leads our youth of both sexes to shun labor; and it is the business of the true teacher to extirpate this growth of a diseased civilization. And we could have no faith in this school, if it were not a school of industry as well as of morality,—a school in which the divine law of labor is to be observed equally with the laws of men. Industry is near to all the virtues. In this era every branch of labor is an art, and sometimes it is necessary for the laborer to be both an artist and a scientific person. How great, then, the misfortune of those, whether rich or poor, who are uninstructed in the business of life! We should hardly know what judgment to pass upon a man of wealth who should entirely neglect the education of his children in schools; but the common indifference to industrial learning is not less reprehensible. Labor should be systematic; not constant, indeed, but always to be reckoned as the great business of life, never to be avoided, never to cease.

Labor gives us a better knowledge of the fulness, magnificence and glory, of the divine blessing of creation. This lesson may be learned by the farmer in the wonderful growth of vegetation; by the artist, in the powers of invention and taste of the human mind and soul; by the man of science, in the beauty of an insect or the order of a universe. The vision of the idle is limited. The ability to see may be improved by education as much as the ability to read, remember, or converse. With many people, not seeing is a habit. Near-sighted persons are generally those who declined to look at distant objects; and so nature, true to the most perfect rules of economy, refused to keep in order faculties that were entirely neglected. The laborer's recompense is not money, nor the accumulation of worldly goods chiefly; but it is in his increased ability to observe, appreciate, and enjoy the world, with its beauties and blessings. Nor is labor, the penalty for sin, a punishment merely, but a divine means of reformation. It is, therefore, a moral discipline that all should submit to; and especially is it a means by which the youth here are to be prepared for the duties of life. But industry is not only near to all the virtues; it is itself a virtue, as idleness is a vice. The word *labor* is, of course, used in the broadest signification. Labor is any honest employment, or use of the head or hands, which brings good to ourselves, and consequently, though indirectly, brings good to our fellow-men.

The state has now furnished a home, reproduced, as far as practicable, the family relation, and provided for a class of neglected and exposed girls the means of mental, industrial, moral, and religious culture. The plan appears well; but its practical value depends upon the fidelity of its execution by the superintendent, matrons and assistants. I venture to predict in advance, that the degree of success is mainly within their control. This is a school, they are the teachers ; and they must bend to the rule which all true teachers willingly accept.

The teacher must be what he would have his pupils become. This was the standard of the great Teacher ; this is the aim of all who desire to make education a matter of reality and life, and not merely a knowledge of signs and forms. Here will be needed a spirit and principle of devotion which will be fruitful in humility, patience, earnestness, energy, good words and works for all. Here must be strictness, possibly sternness of discipline ; but this is not incompatible with the qualities mentioned. It is a principle at Mettray to combine unbounded personal kindness with a rigid exclusion of personal indulgence.

This principle produces good results that are twofold in their influence. First, personal kindness in the teacher induces a reciprocal quality in the pupils. The habit of personal kindness, proceeding from right feelings, is a potent element of good in the family, the school, and the prison. Indeed, it is an element of good citizenship ; and no one destitute of this quality ought to be intrusted with the education of children, or the punishment and reformation of criminals.

Secondly, the rigid exclusion of personal indulgence trains the inmates in the virtue of self-control. And may it not be forgotten that all apparent reformation must be hedged by this cardinal virtue of practical life! Otherwise the best-formed expectations will fail; the highest hopes will be disappointed; and the life of these teachers, and the promise of the youth who may be gathered here, will be like the sun and the winds upon the desert, which bring neither refreshing showers nor fruitful harvests. Every form of labor requires faith. This labor requires faith in yourselves, and faith in others; — faith in yourselves, as teachers here, based upon your own knowledge of what you are and are to do; and faith in others upon the divine declaration that God breathed into man the breath of life, and he became a living soul, — not merely as the previous creations, possessed of animal life; but as a sentient, intellectual, and moral being, capable of a progressive, immortal existence.

> " 'T is nature's law
> That none, the meanest of created things,
> * * * * *
> Should exist
> Divorced from good, — a spirit and pulse of good,

A life and soul, to every mode of being
Inseparably linked.

See, then, your only conflict is with men;
And your sole strife is to defend and teach
The unillumined, who, without such care,
Must dwindle."

And always, as in the beginning, the reliance of this school is upon the people of the commonwealth, whose voice has spoken into existence another instrumentality to give eyes to the blind, ears to the deaf, a heart for the work of this life, and a hope for an hereafter, to those who from neglect and vicious example would soon pass the period of reformation. But may the people always bear in mind the indisputable truth, that schools for the criminal and the exposed yield not their perfect fruits in a day or a year! They must, if they will know whether the seed here planted produces a harvest, wait for the birth and growth of one generation, the decay and death of another. Yet these years of delay will not be years of uncertainty. The public faith will be strengthened continually by cases of reformation, usefulness, and virtue. But, whether these cases be few or many, let no one despond. The career of the criminal is, often in money and always in influence, the heaviest burden which an individual can impose upon society.

This is a school for girls ; and we may properly appeal to the women of Massachusetts to do their duty to this institution, and to the cause it represents. We can already see the second stage in the existence of many of those who are to be sent here ; and there is good reason to fear that the relation of mistress and servant among us is in some degree destitute of those moral qualities that make the house a home for all who dwell beneath its roof. But, whether this fear be the voice of truth or the suggestion of prejudice, that woman shall not be held blameless, who, under the influence of indolence, pride, fashion, or avarice, shall neglect, abuse, or oppress, the humblest of her sex who goes forth from these walls into the broad and dangerous path of life. But this day shall not leave the impression that they who are most interested in the elevation and refinement of female character are indifferent to the means employed, and the results which are to wait on them.

The greatest delineator of human character in this age says, as the images of neglected children pass before his vision :

"There is not one of them — not one — but sows a harvest mankind *must* reap. From every seed of evil in this boy a field of ruin is grown that shall be gathered in, and garnered up, and sown again in many places in the world, until regions are overspread with wickedness enough to raise the waters of another deluge. Open and unpunished murder in a city's streets would be less guilty in its daily toleration than one such spectacle as this. There is not a father, by whose side, in his daily or nightly walk, these creatures pass ; there is not a mother among all the ranks of loving mothers in this land ; there is no one risen from the state of childhood, but shall be responsible, in his or her degree, for this enormity. There is not a country throughout the earth on which it would not bring a curse. There is no religion upon earth that it would not deny ; there is no people on earth that it would not put to shame."

This institution, then, in the true relation of things, is not the glory of the state, but its shame. It speaks of families, of schools, of the church, of the state, not yet educated to the discharge of their respective duties in the right way. But it is the glory of the state as a visible effort to correct evils, atone for neglects, and compensate for wrongs. It comes to do, in part at least, what the family, the school, the press, the library, the Sabbath, have not yet perfectly accomplished. As these agencies partially failed, so will this ; but, as the law of progress exists for all, because perfection with us is unattainable, we may reasonably have faith in human improvement, and trust that the life of each succeeding generation shall unite, in ever-increasing proportions, the innocence of childhood with the wisdom of age.

ELEMENTARY TRAINING IN THE PUBLIC SCHOOLS.

[Extract from the Twenty-Second Annual Report of the Secretary of the Massachusetts Board of Education.]

We are still sadly defective in methods of education. Until recently teaching was almost an unknown art; and we are at present struggling against ignorance without any well-defined plan, and attempting to develop and build up the immortal character of children, without a philosophical and generally accepted theory of the nature of the human mind. There are complaints that the duties and exactions of the schools injure the health and impair the constitutions of pupils; that the progress in intellectual attainments is not always what it should be; that the training given is sometimes determined by the wishes of committees against the better judgment of competent teachers; that the text-books are defective; that the studies in the common schools are too numerous; that the elements are consequently neglected; and that, in fine, too much thought is bestowed upon exhibitions and contests for public prizes, to the injury of good learning, and of individual and general character. For these complaints there is some foundation; but care should be exercised lest incidental and necessary evils become, in the public estimation, great wrongs, and exceptional cases the evidence of general facts.

It is to some extent true that the duties and exactions of the schools seriously test the health of pupils; but it is, as I believe, more generally true that many pupils are physically unable to meet the ordinary and proper duties of the school-room. School life, as usually conducted, is physically injurious, and our best efforts thus far have been limited to the dissemination of elementary knowledge of physiology as a science, and to an acquaintance with a limited number of important physiological facts. Yet even here little has been accomplished in comparison with what may be done. In this department there is much instruction given that has no practical value, and children are often permitted to live in daily and uniform neglect of the most essential truths of science and the facts of human experience. Neither physiology nor hygiene can be of much value in the schools, as a study, unless there is an application of what is taught. Great proficiency cannot be made in these branches in the brief period of school life; but a competent teacher may induce the pupils to put in practice the lessons that are applicable to childhood and youth. If, however, as is sometimes the case, pupils are undermining the physical constitution in their efforts to know how they are made, the loss is, unquestionably, more than the gain. Physical health and growth depend, first, upon opportunity; and hence it happens that, where physical life is most defective, there the greatest difficulties in the way of its improvement are found. Boys, born in the country, living upon farms, accustomed continually to outdoor labors and sports, walking a mile or more every day to school, have but little use, in their own persons, for the science or facts of physiology; and it is a very rare thing, where such conditions have existed, that any teacher is able to exact an amount of intellectual service that proves in any perceptible degree injurious.

But these opportunities are not so generally enjoyed by girls, and the mass of children in cities are wholly deprived of them. In the country, and even in villages and towns of considerable size, there is no excuse, better than ignorance or indifference, for the lack of judicious and efficient physical training of children and youth of both sexes. But ignorance and indifference are facts; and, while and where they exist, they are prejudicial to the growth of mind and body. The age at which children should be admitted to school has not been ascertained, nor can a satisfactory rule upon this point ever be laid down. If children are not in schools, they are yet subject to influences that are formative of character. When proper government and methods of education exist at home, the presence of the child in school at an early age is not desirable. Even when education at home is not methodical, it may be continued until the child is seven or even eight years of age, if it is at once moral, intelligent, and controlling. It is not, however, wise to expect a child who is infirm physically to perform the labors imposed by the necessary and proper regulations of school. When children enjoy good health, and are not blessed with suitable training at home, they may be introduced to the school, at the age of five years, with positive advantage to themselves and to society.

When the child is a member of the school, what shall be done with him? He must first be taught to take an interest in the exercises by making the exercises interesting to him. That the transition from home to the school may be easy, he should first occupy himself with those topics and studies that are presented to the eye and to the ear, and may be mastered, so as to produce the sensation that follows achievement with only a moderate use of the reasoning and reflective faculties. Among these are reading, writing, music, and drawing. This is also the time when object lessons may be given with great advantage. The forms and names of geometrical solids may be taught. Exercises may be introduced tending to develop those powers by which we comprehend the qualities of color, size, density, form, and weight. Important moral truths may be presented with the aid of suitable illustrations. In every school the teacher and text-books may be considered a positive quality which should balance the negative power of the school itself. In primary schools text-books have but little value, and the chief reliance is, therefore, upon the teacher. Instruction must be mainly oral ; hence the mind of the teacher should be well furnished, and her capacities chastened by considerable experience. As the pupils are unable to study, the teacher must lead in all their exercises, and find profitable employment for the children, or they will give themselves up to play or to stupid listlessness. Of these alternatives, the latter is more objectionable than the former.

It is, of course, not often possible for a teacher to occupy herself six hours a day with a single class in a primary school, especially if she confines her attention to the studies enumerated. In many schools, of various grades, gymnastic exercises have been introduced with marked advantage. There are many such exercises which do not need apparatus, and in which the teacher can properly lead.

These furnish a healthful variety to the studies usually pursued, and they prepare the pupils to receive appropriate instruction in sitting, standing, and in the modulation and use of the voice. Indeed, gymnastic exercises are indispensable aids to proper training in reading, which, as an art of a high order, is immediately dependent upon position, habits of breathing, the consequent power of voice, and expressiveness of tone. I am fully satisfied that much more may be done in the early period of school life than is usually accomplished. In the district mixed schools the primary pupils receive but little attention, and they are not infrequently occupied from one to three years in obtaining an imperfect knowledge of the alphabet. Usually much better results are attained by the combined agency of the home and the school, but there is an average loss of one-fourth of the time employed in teaching and learning the elements of our language.

Mr. Philbrick, Superintendent of Public Schools in Boston, has taught and trained a class of fifty primary-school pupils with a degree of success which fully sustains the statement of the average waste in schools generally. Twenty-two lessons of a half-hour each were given; and in this brief period of time the class, with a few exceptions, were so well advanced that they could write the alphabet in capital and script hand, give the elementary sounds of the letters, produce and name the Arabic characters and the common geometrical figures found upon Holbrook's slates. I saw a girl, five and a half years of age, write the alphabet without delay in script hand, in a manner that would have been creditable to a pupil in a grammar school.

I present Mr. Philbrick's own account of his mode of proceeding, in an extract from his third quarterly report to the school committee of the city of Boston.

"The regulations relating to the primary schools require every scholar to be provided with a slate, and to employ the time not otherwise occupied in drawing or writing words from their spelling lessons, on their slates, in a plain script hand. It is further stated, in the same connection, that the teachers are expected to take special pains to teach the first class to write — not print — all the letters of the alphabet on slates.

"The language of this requirement seems to imply that the classes below the first are to draw and write words, in a plain script hand, without any special pains to teach them, and that by such occupation they were to be kept from idleness. As I saw neither of these objects accomplished in any primary school, I thought it worth while to satisfy myself, by actual experiment, what can and ought to be done, in the use of the slate and blackboard, in teaching writing and drawing in primary schools. To accomplish this object, I have given a course of lessons in a graded or classified school of the third class. The number of pupils instructed in the class was about fifty. The materials of the school are rather below the average; about twenty of the pupils being of that description usually found in schools for special instruction. The school-room is furnished, as every primary school-room should be, with stationary chairs and desks, and Holbrook's primary slates. Twenty-two lessons, of from thirty to forty minutes each, were given, about one-third of the time being devoted to drawing, and two-thirds to writing. As to the method pursued, the main points were, to present but a single element at a time; to illustrate on the blackboard defects and excellences in execution; frequent review of the ground passed over, especially in the *first* steps of the course; a vigorous exercise of all the mental faculties requisite for the performance of the task; and a desire for improvement, encouraged and stimulated by the best and strongest available motives;

the greater part of the time being bestowed upon the dull and backward pupils.

"The result has exceeded my expectations. About three-fourths of the number taught can draw most of the simple mathematical lines and figures, given as copies on the slates used, with tolerable accuracy, and write all the letters of the alphabet in a fair script hand. This experiment satisfies me that, with the proper facilities, the three upper classes in graded primary schools can be taught to write the letters of the alphabet in a plain script hand, and even to join them into words, without any material hindrance to the other required studies ; and, moreover, that the great remedy for the complaint of want of time, in these schools, is the increase of skill in the art of teaching."

It is well known that in this country and in Europe methods of teaching the alphabet have been introduced which materially diminish the labor of teachers, and lessen the drudgery to which children are usually subjected. The alphabet is taught as an object lesson. The object is usually an animal, plant, or flower. More frequently the first. The mind of the child is awakened either by the presence of the animal, or by a brief but vivid description of its characteristics. The children are first required to pronounce properly the name of the animal. Here is an opportunity for training in the use of the voice, and in the art of breathing, with which the general health, as well as the vocal power, is intimately connected. The word which is the name of the animal is analyzed into its elementary sounds. It may then be reconstructed without the aid of visible signs, either written or printed. Next the teacher produces the signs which stand for the several sounds, and gives their names. The letters are presented in any way that suits the teacher. There may be no better method than to produce them upon the blackboard, as this course encourages the pupils to draw them upon their slates, and thus they are at once, and without formal preliminaries, engaged in writing.

An outline of the animal may be drawn upon the blackboard, which the pupils will eagerly copy; and though this exercise may not be valuable in a high degree, as preparation for the systematic study of drawing, yet it trains the perceptive and reflective faculties in a manner that is pleasant to the great majority of children. It is also in the power of the teacher, at any point in the exercises, and with reference both to variety and usefulness, to give the most apparent facts, which to children are the most interesting facts, in the natural history of the animal. This plan contemplates instruction in pronunciation in connection with exercises in breathing, in the elementary sounds of words both consonant and vowel, in the names of letters, in writing and drawing, to all of which may be added something of natural history. It is of course to be understood that such exercises would be extended over many lessons, be subject to frequent reviews, and valuable in proportion to the teacher's ability to interest children. The outline given is suggestive, merely, and it is not presented as a plan of a model course ; but enough has been done and is doing in this department to warrant increased attention, and to justify the belief that a degree of progress will soon be made in teaching the elements that will mark the epoch as a revolution in educational affairs. It is to be observed that the system indicated requires a high order of teaching talent. Only thorough professional culture, or long and careful experience, will meet the claims of such a course. It is quite plain, however, that no advantage would arise from keeping pupils in school six hours each day ; and that, regarding only the intellectual advancement of the child during the elementary course, his presence might be reduced to two hours, or possibly in some cases to one : provided, always, that he could enjoy, with his class associates, the undivided attention of the teacher. In this view of the subject, it would be possible, where the primary schools are graded, as in portions of the city of Boston, for one teacher to take charge of two classes or schools, each for an hour in the forenoon and an hour in the afternoon. This arrangement would apply only to the younger pupils; yet I am aware that parents and the public would be solicitous concerning the manner of employing the time that would remain. In the cities this question is one of magnitude, and there are strong reasons for declining any proposition to reduce the school day full one-half, which does not provide occupation for the children during the remainder of the time. It is only in connection with such a proposition that projects for gymnastic training are practicable. When children are employed six hours in school, it is not easy to find time for a course of systematic physical education; and physical education, to be productive of appreciable advantages, must be systematic. When left to children and youth, or to the care of parents, very little will be accomplished. Children will participate in the customary sports, and perform the allotted labors; but in cities these sports and labors are inadequate even for boys, and in country, as well as city, girls are often the victims of neglect in this respect. Availing ourselves, then, of the light shed by recent experience upon the subject of primary instruction, it seems possible to diminish the length of the school day with a gain rather than a loss of educational power. This change may be followed by the establishment, in cities and large towns, of public gymnasiums, where teachers answering in moral qualifications to the requisitions of the laws shall be employed, and where each child, for one, two, or three years, shall receive discreet and careful, but vigorous physical training. After a few years thus passed in corresponding and healthful development of the mind and body, the pupil is prepared for admission to the advanced schools, where he can submit, with perfect safety, to greater mental requirements even than are now made. The school, as at present constituted, cannot do much for physical education ; and it must, as a necessity and a duty, graduate its demands to the physical as well as the intellectual abilities of its pupils. But I am satisfied that it is occasionally made to bear a weight of reproach that ought to be laid upon the customs and habits of domestic, social and general life.

Assuming that the principal work of the primary schools, after moral and physical culture, should be to give instruction in reading, spelling, writing, music and drawing, it is just to say that special attention should be bestowed upon the two branches first named. So imperfectly is reading sometimes taught, that pupils are found in advanced classes, and in advanced schools, whose progress in other branches is retarded by their inability to read the language fluently and intelligently. When children are well educated in reading, they find profitable employment; and they are, of course, by the knowledge of language acquired, able to comprehend, with greater facility, every study to which they are called.

Pupils often appear dull in grammar, geography and arithmetic, merely because they are poor readers. A child is not qualified to use a text-book of any science until he is able to read with facility, as we are accustomed to speak, in groups of words. This ability he cannot acquire without a great deal of practice. If phonetic spelling is commenced with the alphabet, he will be accurately trained in that art also. It is certain that reading, writing and spelling, have been neglected in our schools generally.

If there is to be a reform, it must be commenced, and in a considerable degree accomplished, in the primary schools. These studies will be taught afterwards; but the grammar and high schools can never compensate for any defect permitted, or any wrong done, in the primary schools. Reading is first mechanical, and then intellectual and emotional. In the primary schools attention is first given to mechanical training, while the intellectual and emotional culture is necessarily in a degree postponed. When the first part of the work is thoroughly done, there is no ground for complaint, and we may look to the teachers of advanced classes and schools for the proper performance of the remaining duty. The ability to spell arbitrarily, either in writing or orally, and the ability to read mechanically,—that is, the ability to seize the words readily, and utter them fluently and accurately, — must be acquired by much spelling and much reading.

This work belongs to the early years of school-life ; and, if it can be faithfully performed, the introduction of text-books in grammar, geography and arithmetic, may be wisely postponed. But it is a sad condition of things, which we are often compelled to contemplate, when a pupil, who might have become a respectable reader had the elementary training been careful, accurate and long-continued, is introduced to an advanced class, and there struggles against obstacles which he cannot comprehend, and which the teacher cannot remove, and finally leaves the school without the ability to read in a manner intelligible to himself, or satisfactory to others. It is the appropriate work of primary schools, and of the teachers of primary classes in district schools, to develop and chasten the moral powers of children, to train them in those habits and practices that are favorable to health and life, whether anything is known of physiology as a science or not, and to give the best culture possible to the eye, the ear, the hand and the voice. This plan is comprehensive enough for any teacher, and it will be found sufficient for any pupil less than ten years of age. Nor am I speaking of that culture which is merely preparatory for the life of the artist, but of that practical training which will enable the subject of it so to use his powers as to render his life valuable to himself, and valuable to the world. There will be, in the exercises comprehended by this outline, sufficient mental discipline. It will, of course, be chiefly incidental, and it may well be doubted whether studies that are merely disciplinary should ever be introduced into our schools. There are useful occupations for pupils that, at the same time, tax and test the mind sufficiently. The plan indicated does not exclude grammar, geography and mental arithmetic, but text-books will not at first be needed. Grammar should be taught by conversation, and in connection with the exercises in reading. Grammar is the appreciation of the power of the words of the language in any given relations to each other, and a knowledge of grammar is essential to the ability to speak, read and write properly. Therefore, grammatical rules and definitions are, or should be, deduced from the language. Hence children should be first trained to speak with accuracy, so that habit shall be on the side of taste and science; next the offices which words perform in simple sentences should be illustrated and made clear. And thus far without text-books; when, finally, with their help, the pupils in the higher schools may acquire a knowledge of the science, and, at once, as the result of previous training, discern the reason for each rule and definition. The study of grammar requires some use of mental power; but when it is presented to pupils by the aid of an object which, in itself and in what it does, illustrates the subject and the predicate of a sentence, the work of comprehending the offices which words perform is rendered comparatively easy. Having the skeleton thus furnished, and with the eyes and minds of the pupils fixed upon an object that possesses known and appreciable powers and qualities, it is not difficult for the teacher to construct a sentence that shall contain words of several parts of speech, all understood, because the grammatical office of each was seen even before the word itself was used. This work may be commenced when the child is young, and very satisfactory results ought to be secured as soon as the pupil is in other respects qualified to enter a grammar school. The pupil should be trained in reading as an art; that is, with the purpose of expressing whatever is intellectual and emotional in the text. Satisfactory results cannot at first be secured by much reading; it seems wiser for the teacher to select an extract, paragraph, or single sentence only, and drill a pupil or a class until the meaning of the author is comprehended, and accurately or even artistically expressed. This can be done only when the teacher reads the passage again and again in the best manner possible. The contrary practice of reading volumes of extracts from the writings of the most gifted men of ancient and modern times, without preparation by the pupil, without example, explanation, correction, or questionings, by the teacher, cannot be too strongly condemned. The time will come when these selections may be read with profit; but it is better to read something well than to read a great deal; or there should be at least thorough drill in connection with every exercise, until the pupils have attained some degree of perfection. It may not be best to confine advanced pupils to the exercises in the text-books. If such pupils are invited occasionally to make selections from their entire range of reading, the teacher will have an opportunity to correct whatever is vicious in taste; and the pupil making the selection will be compelled to read in such a manner that those who listen can understand, which is not always the case when the language is addressed to the eye as well as to the ear.

The introduction of Colburn's Intellectual Arithmetic was an epoch in the science. It wrought a radical change in the ability of the people to apply the power of numbers to the practical business of life. Its excellence does not consist in rules and illustrations by which examples and problems are easily solved, but in leading the mind of the pupil into natural and apparent processes of reasoning, by which he is enabled to comprehend a proposition as an independent fact. Herein is a mental discipline of great value, not only in the sciences, but in the daily affairs of men of all classes and conditions. It is to be feared that equally satisfactory results have not been attained in what is called written arithmetic. This partial failure deserves consideration. The first cause may be found in an erroneous opinion concerning the difference between mental and written arithmetic. Written arithmetic is mental arithmetic merely, with a record at given stages of the process of what at that point is accomplished. But, as written arithmetic tends to lessen the power of the pupil for the performance of those operations that are purely mental, he should be subjected, each day, to a searching and rapid drill in mental arithmetic also. This neglect on the part of teachers explains the singular fact that pupils, well trained in mental arithmetic, after attending to written arithmetic for three or six months, appear to have lost rather than gained in their knowledge of the science as a whole.

The second cause of failure may be found in the fact that rules, processes and simple methods of solution, contained in the books, are substituted for the power of comprehension by the pupil. He should be trained to seize an example mentally, whether the slate is to be used or not, and hold it until he can determine by what process the solution is to be wrought. Nor is it a serious objection that he may not at first avail himself of the easiest method. The difference between methods or ways is altogether a subordinate consideration. There may be many ways of reaching a truth, but no one of them is as important as the truth itself. The text-books should contain all the facts needed for the comprehension and the solution of the examples given ; the teacher should furnish explanations and other aids, as they are needed; but the practice of adopting a process and following it to an apparently satisfactory conclusion, without comprehending the problem itself, is a serious educational evil, and it exerts a permanent pernicious influence.

The remarks I have now made upon methods of teaching, which may seem to have been offered in a spirit of severe criticism, should be qualified and relieved by the statement that our teachers are as well educated as any in the country, and that they are yearly making progress in their profession. Indeed, I am encouraged to suggest that better things are possible, by the consideration that many instances of distinguished success in teaching the alphabet, reading and grammar, are known to me; and that teachers are themselves aware that the work is, upon the whole, inadequately performed. If, as is generally conceded, the highest order of teaching talent is required in the primary schools, then that talent should be sought out by committees; the persons possessing it should enjoy the best means of preparation; they should receive the highest rewards, both in money and public consideration, and they should be induced to labor, without change or interruption, in the same schools and among the same people.

THE RELATIVE MERITS OF PUBLIC HIGH SCHOOLS AND ENDOWED ACADEMIES.

[Remarks before the American Institute of Instruction, at Manchester, N. H.]

INDEBTED to my friend on the other side, and to you, sir, and this audience, for inviting me to take a position on this floor, I am still without any special preparation to discuss the subject. I have thought upon it, because any one, however humbly connected with free schools in this country, must have done so. And especially just now, when, in the educational journal of Massachusetts, a discussion has been conducted between one of its editors and Mr. Gulliver, the able originator of a school in Norwich, Ct., and the advocate of the system of school government established there. And, therefore, every one who has had his eyes open must have seen that here is a great contest, and that underlying it is a principle which is important to society.

The distinguishing difference between the advocates of endowed schools and of free schools is this: those who advocate the system of endowed academies go back in their arguments to one foundation, which is, that in education of the higher grades the great mass of the people are not to be trusted. And those who advocate a system of free education in high schools put the matter where we have put the rights of property and liberty, where we put the institutions of law and religion — upon the public judgment. And we will stand there. If the public will not maintain institutions of learning, then, I say, let institutions of learning go down. If I belong to a state which cannot be moved from its extremities to its centre, and from its centre to its extremities, for the maintenance of a system of public instruction, then, in that respect, I disown that state; and if there be one state in this Union whose people cannot be aroused to maintain a system of public instruction, then they are false to the great leading idea of American principles, and of civil, political, and religious liberty.

It is easy to enumerate the advantages of a system of public education, and the evils — I say evils — of endowed academies, whether free or charging payment for tuition. Endowed academies are not, in all respects, under all circumstances, and everywhere, to be condemned. In discussing this subject, it may be well for me to state the view that I have of the proper position of endowed academies. They have a place in the educational wants of this age. This is especially true of academies of the highest rank, which furnish an elevated and extended course of instruction. To such I make no objection, but I would honor and encourage them. Yet I regard private schools, which do the work usually done in public schools, as temporary, their necessity as ephemeral, and I think that under a proper public sentiment they will soon pass away. They cannot stand, — such has been the experience in Massachusetts, — they cannot stand by the side of a good system of public education. Yet where the population is sparse, where there is not property sufficient to enable the people to establish a high school, then an endowed school may properly come in to make up the deficiency, to supply the means of education to which the public wealth, at the present moment, is unequal. Endowed institutions very properly, also, give a professional education to the people. At this moment we cannot look to the public to give that education which is purely professional. But what we do look to the public for is this : to furnish the means of education to the children of the whole people, without any reference to social, pecuniary, political, or religious distinctions, so that every person may have a preliminary education sufficient for the ordinary business of life.

It is said that the means of education are better in

an endowed academy, or in an endowed free school, than they can be in a public school. What is meant by *means* of education? I understand that, first and chiefly, as extraneous means of education, we must look to a correct public sentiment, which shall animate and influence the teacher, which shall give direction to the school, which shall furnish the necessary public funds. An endowed free academy can have none of these things permanently. Take, for example, the free school established at Norwich by the liberality of thirty or forty gentlemen, who contributed ninety thousand dollars. What security is there that fifty years hence, when the educational wants of the people shall be changed, when the population of Norwich shall be double or treble what it is now, when science shall make greater demands, when these forty contributors shall have passed away, this institution will answer the wants of that generation? According to what we know of the history of this country, it will be entirely inadequate; and, though none of us may live to see the prediction fulfilled or falsified, I do not hesitate to say that the school will ultimately prove a failure, because it is founded in a mistake.

Then look and see what would have been the state of things if there had been public spirit invoked to establish a public high school, and if the means for its support had been raised by taxation of all the people, so that the system of education would have expanded according to the growth of the city, and year by year would have accommodated itself to the public wants and public zeal in the cause. Though these means seem now to be ample, they will by and by be found too limited. The school at Norwich is encumbered with regulations; and so every endowed institution is likely to be, because the right of a man to appropriate his property to a particular object carries with it, in the principles of common law, and in the administration of the law, in all free governments, the right to declare, to a certain extent, how that property shall be applied. Rules have been established — very proper and judicious rules for to-day. But who knows that a hundred years hence they will be proper or acceptable at all? They have also established a board of trustees, ultimately to be reduced to twenty-five. These trustees have power to perpetuate themselves. Who does not see that you have severed this institution from the public sentiment of the city of Norwich, and that ultimately that city will seek for itself what it needs; and that, a hundred years hence, it will not consent to live, in the civilization of that time, under the regulations which forty men have now established, however wise the regulations may at the present moment be?

One hundred and fifty years ago, Thomas Hollis, of London, made a bequest to the university at Cambridge, with a provision that on every Thursday a professor should sit in his chair to answer questions in polemic theology. All well enough then; but the public sentiment of to-day will not carry it out.

So it may be with the school at Norwich a hundred years hence. The man or state that sacrifices the living public judgment to the opinion of a dead man, or a dead generation, makes a great mistake. We should never substitute, beyond the power of revisal, the opinion of a past generation for the opinion of a living generation. I trust to the living men of to-day as to what is necessary to meet our existing wants, rather than to the wisest men who lived in Greece or Rome. And, if I would not trust the wise men of Greece and Rome, I do not know why the people, a hundred years hence, should trust the wise men of our own time.

And then look further, and see how, under a system of public instruction, you can build up, from year to year, in the growth of the child, a system according to his wants. Private instruction cannot do this. What do we do where we have a correct system? A child goes into a primary school. He is not to go out when he attains a certain age. He might as well go out when he is of a certain height; there would be as much merit in one case as in the other. But he is advanced when he has made adequate attainments. Who does not see that the child is incited and encouraged and stimulated by every sentiment to which you should appeal? And, then, when he has gone up to the grammar school, we say to him, "You are to go into the high school when you have made certain attainments." And who is to judge of these attainments? A committee appointed by the people, over whom the people have some ultimate control. And in that control they have security for two things: first, that the committee shall not be suspected of partiality; and secondly, that they shall not be actually guilty of partiality. In the same manner, there is security for the proper connection between the high school and the schools below. But in the school at Norwich — of which I speak because it is now prominent — you have a board of twenty-five men, irresponsible to the people. They select a committee of nine; that committee determines what candidates shall be transferred from the grammar schools to the high school. May there not be suspicion of partiality? If a boy or girl is rejected, you look for some social, political, or religious influence which has caused the rejection, and the parent and child complain. Here is a great evil; for the real and apparent justice of the examination and decision by which pupils are transferred from one school to another is vital to the success of the system.

There is another advantage in the system of public high schools, which I imagine the people do not always at first appreciate. It is, that the private school, with the same teachers, the same apparatus, and the same means, cannot give the education which may be, and usually is, furnished in the public schools. This statement may seem to require some considerable support. We must look at facts as they are. Some people are poor; I am sorry for them. Some people are rich, and I congratulate them upon their good fortune. But it is not so much of a benefit, after all, as many think. It is worth something in this world, no doubt, to be rich; but what is the result of that condition upon the family first, the school afterwards, and society finally? It is, that some learn the lesson of life a little earlier than others; and that lesson is the lesson of self-reliance, which is worth more than — I will not say a knowledge of the English language — but worth more than Latin or Greek. If the great lesson of self-reliance is to be learned, who is more likely to acquire it early, — the child of the poor, or the child of the rich; the child who has most done for him, or the child who is under the necessity of doing most for himself? Plainly, the latter. Now, while a system of public instruction in itself cannot be magnified in its beneficial influences to the poor and to the children of the poor, it is equally beneficial to the rich in the facility it affords for the instruction of their children. Is it not worth something to the rich man, who cannot, from the circumstances of the case, teach self-reliance around the family hearth, to send his child to school to learn this lesson with other children, that he may be stimulated, that he may be provoked to exertions which he would not otherwise have made? For, be it remembered that in our schools public sentiment is as well marked as in a college, or a town, or a nation; that it moves forward in the same way. And the great object of a teacher should be to create a public sentiment in favor of virtue. There should be some pioneers in favor of forming a correct public sentiment; and when it is formed it moves on irresistibly. It is like the river made up of drops from the mountain side, moving on with more and more power, until everything in its waters is carried to the destined end.

So in a public school. And it is worth much to the man of wealth that there may be, near his own door, an institution to which he may send his children, and under the influence of which they may be carried forward. For, depend upon it, after all we say about schools and institutions of learning, it is nevertheless true of education, as a statesman has said of the government, that the people look to the school for too much. It is not, after all, a great deal that the child gets there; but, if he only gets the ability to acquire more than he has, the schools accomplish something. If you give a child a little knowledge of geography or arithmetic, and have not developed the power to accomplish something for himself, he comes to but little in the world. But put him into the school, — the primary, grammar, and high school, where he must learn for himself, — and he will be fitted for the world of life into which he is to enter.

You will see in this statement that, with the same parties, the same means of education, the same teachers, the public schools will accomplish more than private schools.

I find everywhere, and especially in the able address of Mr. Gulliver, to which I have referred, that the public schools are treated as of questionable morality, and it is implied that something would be gained by removing certain children from the influence of these schools. If I were speaking from another point of view, very likely I should feel bound to hold up the evils and defects which actually exist in public schools; but when I consider them in contrast with endowed and private schools, I do not hesitate to say that the public schools compare favorably; and, as the work of education goes on, the comparison will be more and more to their advantage. Why? I know something of the private institutions in Massachusetts; and there are boys in them who have left the public schools because they have fallen in their classes, and the public interest would not justify their continuance in the schools. It was always true that private schools did not represent the world exactly as it was. It is worth everything to a boy or girl, man or woman, to look the world in the face as it is.

Therefore, the public school, when it represents the world as it is, represents the facts of life. The private school never has done and never will do this; and as time goes on, it will be less and less a true representative of the world. From this point of view, it seems to be a mistake on the part of parents to exclude their children from the world. Is it not better that the child should learn something of society, even of its evils, when under your influence, and when you can control him by your counsel and example, than to permit him finally to go out, as you must when his majority comes, perhaps to be seduced in a moment, as it were, from his allegiance to virtue? Virtue is not exclusion from the presence of vice; but it is resistance to vice in its presence. And it is the duty of parents to provide safeguards for the support of their children against these temptations. When Cicero was called on to defend Muræna against the slander that, as he had lived in Asia, he had been guilty of certain crimes, and when the testimony failed to substantiate the charge, the orator said, "And if Asia does carry with it a suspicion of luxury, surely it is a praiseworthy thing, not never to have seen Asia, but to have lived temperately in Asia." And we have yet higher authority. It is not the glory of Christ, or of Christianity, that its Divine Author was without temptation, but that, being tempted, he was without sin. This is the great lesson of the day.

The duty of the public is to provide means for the education of all. To do that, we need the political, social, and moral power of all, to sustain teachers and institutions of learning; and endowed or free schools, depending upon the contributions of individuals, can never, in a free country, be raised to the character of a system. If you rob the public schools of the influence of our public-spirited men, if they take away a portion of their pupils from them, our system is impaired. It must stand as a whole, educating the entire people, and looking to all for support, or it cannot be permanently maintained.

THE HIGH SCHOOL SYSTEM.

[An Address delivered at the Dedication of the Powers Institute, Bernardston.]

THERE cannot be a more gratifying spectacle than the universal homage offered to education and to the young. Childhood is attractive in itself; and it is peculiarly an object of solicitude for its promises concerning the future. Hence the labors of philanthropists, reformers, and Christians, as well as of teachers, are devoted to the culture and improvement of the rising generation, as the chief security possible for the prevalence of better ideas in the state and in the world.

Massachusetts has been peculiarly favored in the means of education; and we ought ever to recognize the divine influence in the wisdom which led our fathers to lay the foundations of a system that contemplated the education of the whole people. The power of this great idea, universal education, has not been limited to Massachusetts; the states of the West, the states of the South, receive it as the basis of a wise public policy; and had our ancestors contributed nothing else to the glory of the republic, they would yet be entitled to the distinguished consideration of every age and people. The vigor of our culture and the hardihood of our institutions are more manifest out of Massachusetts than in it. The immigrant in his new home in the great valley of prairies, on the northern shores of the American lakes, in Oregon, California, or the islands of the Pacific, invokes the spirit of New England in the establishment of a free church and a free school. And in the spirit and discipline of New England, the thoughts of her sons are turned homeward in adversity, seeking consolation at the sources of early, vigorous, and happy life; or, in prosperity, that they may offer, in gratitude to man and to God, some tribute, always noble, however humble, to the principles and institutions that first formed their characters, and then controlled their destiny; or, in old age, the wanderer, like Jacob in Egypt, with his blessing upon the tribes and families of men, says, "I am to be gathered unto my people; bury me with my fathers." This occasion and its honors are due to the memory of him whose name this institution bears; and his last will and testament is an illustration, or rather the cause, of these prefatory remarks. As the reasonably extended and eminently prosperous life of your wise benefactor approached its close, he, in the principles of Old

England and of New England, ordered and directed the payment of all his just debts ; and then, secondly, expressed the wish, "if practicable, to be buried by the side of his parents in the cemetery at Bernardston." First justice, and then affection for parents, kindred, and home, animated the vital, never-dying soul, as the life of the body ebbed and flowed, and flowed and ebbed, to flow no more. For every good the ancients imagined and named a divinity ; and there is in every good something divine.

We do not deify the living nor the dead ; yet such foundations and institutions as the Lawrence Scientific School, the Peabody Institute, the Powers Institute, will bear to a grateful posterity a knowledge of the virtues of their respective founders, and of the exactness, rectitude, and wisdom, of the public sentiment which religiously consecrates the means provided to the ends proposed.

But just eulogy of the dead is the appropriate duty of those who were the associates and friends of the founder of this school. — It will be my purpose, in the humble part I take in the services of this honored occasion, to point out, as I may be able, the connection between learning and wisdom, and then, by the aid of some general remarks upon education, to examine the fitness of this foundation, and the rules here established, to promote human progress and virtue.

The actual available power of a state is in its adult population ; but its hope is in the classes of children and youth whose plastic minds yield to good influences, and are moulded to higher forms of beauty than have been conceived by Italian or Grecian art. Excellence is always adorable and to be adored. If it appear in beauty of person, it commands our admiration ; and how much more ought wisdom, which is the beauty of the mind and the excellency of the soul, to be cultivated and cherished by every human being! "For what is there, O, ye gods!" says Cicero, "more desirable than wisdom? What more excellent and lovely in itself? What more useful and becoming for a man? Or what more worthy of his reasonable nature?"

But wisdom cannot be acquired in a day, nor without devotion and toil. It is the achievement of a life. It is to be pursued carefully through schools, colleges, and the world, — to be mastered by study, intense thought, rigid mental discipline, and an extensive acquaintance with the best authors of ancient and modern times. It is not the child of ease, indolence, or luxury ; and it is well that it is not. The best of human possessions are cheapened when their attainment is no longer difficult. The wealth of California and Australia has made silver, as an article of luxury, the rival of gold; and the pearl loses its beauty when the mountain streams are as fertile as the depths of the sea. Wisdom comprehends learning, but learning is often found where wisdom is wanting. Wisdom is not accomplishment in study, or perfection in art, or supremacy in poetry or eloquence. Learning is essential to wisdom, for we cannot imagine a wise man who is not also a learned man; and the extent and soundness of his learning may be a measure of his wisdom. Wisdom must always have a basis of learning, but learning is not always a basis of wisdom. Learning is a knowledge of particulars, of details; wisdom is such a combination of these particulars as enables us to harmonize our lives with the laws of nature and of God.

Learning is manifested in what we know; wisdom in what we are, based upon what we know. Philosophy, even, is love for wisdom rather than wisdom itself. The old philosophers defined wisdom to be "the knowledge of things, both divine and human, together with the causes on which they depend;" and in the proverb of Solomon, "The fear of the Lord is the instruction of wisdom." Purity, truth, and justice, are also of its foundation. Wise men of the Jewish and Pagan world built on this foundation, and the Christian can build on none other. Having combined learning with these essential virtues, a liberal, symmetrical, comprehensive character may be built up. In the formation of such a character, industry, powers of observation, strength of will and intellectual humility, are requisite. The virtue and the glory of industry cannot be presented too often to the young. I know of no worldly good or human excellence that can be attained without it; nor is there any inherited possession of name, or wealth, or position, that can be preserved in its extent and quality without active, systematic, judicious labor.

It is not necessary to consider industry as habitual diligence in a pursuit, manual or intellectual; but rather as a judicious arrangement of business and recreation, so as always to have time for the necessary duties of life. Mere diligence is not industry in a good sense; it is labor in a bad sense. Our time should be systematically appropriated to our employments, and each measure of time should be equal to the work or duty appointed for it. Moreover, each work or duty should be accomplished in its appointed time; and this can be secured only by a strong will. The power of will admits of education, culture, improvement, as much as any faculty of the mind or quality of character.

A fickle, planless life cannot accomplish much. System in our plans, and firmness of will in their execution, will place us beyond the reach of ordinary disasters; yet how often do young men go through a course of school studies without a plan, even for the moment, and enter upon life the slaves of chance, the victims of what they call fortune, while they might by industry, system and firmness of will, rise superior to circumstances, and extort a measure of success not unworthy of a noble ambition!

Idleness is a wasting disease, a consuming fire, a destroying demon; in youth it is a calamity, in the vigor of manhood it is a disgrace and a sin, and in old age it can be honorably accepted only as the symbol of reflective leisure earned by a life of industry and virtue. Industry is a badge of honor, an introduction everywhere to the true nobility of the world, the security that each may take of the future for his own happiness and prosperity in it.

Cardinal, personal virtues shrink and wither, or are blasted and die, in the company of idleness; and, without firmness of will, the noblest principles and purest sentiments sometimes wear the livery of vice, and often they give encouragement to it. Good principles, good purposes, good ideas, are made fruitful by a strong resolution; while without it they are like bubbles of water, brilliant in the sun-light, but destined to collapse by the changing, silent force of the medium in which they float. And can any life, not positively vicious and criminal, be less desirable than that of the young man who quietly accepts whatever condition circumstances assign to him? I speak now of his moral and intellectual condition rather than of his social position among men. The latter is not in itself important, and only becomes so through the exhibition of high qualities of mind and character. Social and political consideration we cannot demand as a right; but we may acquire knowledge, develop qualities of character, give evidences of wisdom that entitle us to the respect of our fellows.

It may be agreeable, but it is not absolutely essential, for us to enjoy the public confidence, or even the public consideration; though we can be happy ourselves only when we are conscious of not being totally unworthy. But no social or political concession or consideration is acceptable to a noble mind, that is grudgingly yielded or doubtingly bestowed; and the lustre of great intellects is dimmed when they become subservient to claims that they despise.

But can we acquire a knowledge of things, either divine or human, unless we cultivate our powers of observation? Partial or inaccurate observation, especially of natural things, is a great defect of character ; and in New England, where the aim of educators and of the public in matters of education is elevated, a remedy for this defect ought at once to be sought and applied. Our ideas are vague concerning many subjects of common sight and common observation. Is adult life, even among the educated classes, equal to a description of the common animals, trees, fruits and flowers? Who will paint with words the elm or the oak so that its species will be known while the name is withheld? The introduction of drawing into the schools will improve the power of observation among the people, especially if the pupils are required to make nature their model. And this should always be done. O, how is education belittled and the mind dwarfed by those teachers who keep their pupils' thoughts upon signs and definitions, when they ought to deal continually with the facts, things and life of the world! It is no fable that a student of the higher mathematics, when his master, a practical engineer upon the Boston water-works, required his services, exclaimed, "I had no idea that you had sines and tangents out of doors." With such,

> "Nothing goes for sense or light
> That will not with old rules jump right ;
> As if rules were not in the schools
> Derived from truth, but truth from rules."

And Butler, in his satirical description of Sir Hudibras, ascribes to his hero more practical philosophy than he appears to have intended, and more, certainly, than is found in some modern systems of education:

"In mathematics he was greater
Than Tycho Brahe or Erra Pater;
For he, by geometric scale,
Could take the size of pots of ale;
Resolve by sines and tangents straight,
If bread or butter wanted weight;
And wisely tell what hour o' th' day
The clock does strike, by algebra."

Another prerequisite of wisdom is intellectual humility. Solomon says, "Before honor is humility;" and humility is before wisdom, and even before learning. We ought not to be ashamed of involuntary ignorance. Franklin, when asked how he came to know so much, replied, "By never being ashamed to ask a question."

It is idle for any one to imagine that there is nothing more for him to learn. Indeed, such a theory is good evidence of defective education and limited attainments, if not of a defective mental and moral structure.

Naturalists delight and instruct their pupils and auditors with the wonderful truths folded in the flower, garnered in the plant, or imprisoned in the rock. Yet how much more there must be of God's wisdom in the humblest of the beings created in his image! There are distinctions among men; and out of these distinctions come the truth and the necessity that each may be both a teacher and a pupil of every other. No man, however learned he may be, does know or can know all that is known by his neighbor, though that neighbor be the humblest of shepherds or of fishermen. We are not independent of each other in anything. The earnest and faithful disciple of wisdom goes through life everywhere diffusing knowledge, and everywhere gathering it up. Over the great gateway of life is the inscription, "None but learners enter here;" and along its paths and in its groves are tablets, on which is written, "None but learners sojourn here." He is a poor teacher who is not a learner, and he is but little of a learner who is not something of a teacher also. The best teachers are they who are pupils, and the best pupils are already teachers. Such was the real and avowed character of the great teachers of antiquity; such is the best practice of modern continental Europe, and such is the requirement of nature in all ages. He who does not learn cannot teach. Socrates professed to know only this, that he knew nothing. Plato was a disciple of Socrates and Euclid ; a pupil in the school of Pythagoras ; and, as a traveller, under the disguise of a merchant and a seller of oil, he visited Egypt, and thus gained a knowledge of astronomy, and added something to his learning in other departments. He numbered among his pupils Isocrates, Lycurgus, Aristotle, and Demosthenes ; and for eight years Alexander the Great was the pupil of Aristotle, while Demosthenes

> "Wielded at will that fierce Democratie,
> Shook the arsenal, and fulmined over Greece
> To Macedon, and Artaxerxes' throne."

Thus we trace Demosthenes and Alexander, the master spirits in the struggle of Grecian independence against Macedonian supremacy, through teachers and culture up to Socrates, the wanderer in the streets, and the disturber of the peace of Athens.

It is stated that a distinguished modern philosopher often says, "I don't know," when the curiosity or science of his pupils suggests questions that he has not considered. If we respect and admire the wisdom of the wise, how ought we to be humbled, intellectually, by the reflection that the unknown far exceeds the known, and that all become as little children when they enter the temple of the sages! The ancients prized schools, teachers, and learning, because they were essential to wisdom; and wisdom enabled them to live temperately, justly, and happily, in the present world; while we prize schools, teachers, and learning, because they contribute to what we call success in life. The population of New England is composed of skilful artisans, intelligent merchants, shrewd or eloquent lawyers, industrious and intelligent farmers; and to these results our system of education is too exclusively subservient. These results are not to be condemned, nor are the processes by which they are secured to be neglected. But our schools ought to do something always and for every one, for the full development of a character that is essential to artisans, merchants, lawyers, or farmers. Learning should not be prized merely as an aid to the daily work of life,—though this it properly is and ever ought to be, —but for its expansive power in the mind and soul, by which we attain to a more perfect knowledge of things human and divine. There are many persons who accomplish satisfactorily the tasks assigned them, but who do not always comprehend the processes of life, in its political, social, literary, scientific and industrial relations, by which the affairs of the world are guided.

Something of this is due, speaking of America, and especially of New England, to the universal desire to be engaged in active business. Young men destined for the farm or the shop, the counting-house or the store, leave home and school so early that their apprenticeship is ended long before their majority commences ; and they are thus prepared to enter early and vigorously upon the business of life. This course has its advantages, and it is also attended by many evils. Our youth have but little opportunity for observation, and a great deal of time for experience. They fall into mistakes that should have been observed, and consequently shunned. Moreover, this custom tends to make business men too exclusively and rigidly technical and professional; that is, in plain language, speaking relatively, they know too much of their own vocation, and too little of everything else. Business life follows so closely upon home life and school life, that the lessons of the latter fail to exert an immediate and controlling influence, and it is often only in maturer years that the fruits of early training are seen. The connection is such that the boy or youth becomes a devotee of business before he is developed into complete manhood. This is movement, but not true progress ; activity, but not culture ; appropriation and accumulation, but not natural development.

This peculiarity is less prominent in England, and it is hardly known in the central states of Europe. It is to some extent a national, and especially is it a New England characteristic. It is a manifestation of the forward moving spirit of our people, and it is also at once a promise and the security for the ultimate supremacy of the American race and nation in the affairs of the world. In Athens young men attained their majority when they were sixteen; but they usually prosecuted their studies afterwards, and Aristotle thought them unfit for marriage until they were thirty-seven years of age. This rule was observed by Aristotle in his own case; but we are unable to say whether the rule was made before or after his marriage, which is a fact of much importance when we consider the wisdom of the precept, and the real principles and philosophy of its famous author. Moreover, regardless of one-half of creation, he has neither stated the age at which females are marriageable, nor given us that of his own wife. This neglect justly detracts from his authority; and it will not be strange if young men and women view with distrust an opinion that is so manifestly partial and one-sided. If schools make merely learned people, in a narrow and technical sense, they are not doing their whole work. Such learning makes an efficient population, which is certainly desirable ; but it ought also to be a well-educated population in a broad, comprehensive, philosophic sense. By the force of nature and the developing influences of society, including the church, the school, and the home, we ought first to be educated men and women, and then apply that education to the particular work we have in hand. By learning, in this connection, I do not mean the learning of Agassiz as a naturalist, the learning of Choate as a lawyer, or the learning of Everett as an orator ; but a more general and less minute culture, by which men are prepared to form an accurate judgment upon subjects that usually attract public attention.

In the gardens of the wealthy, we often see peach-trees and pear-trees trained against brick or stone walls, to which they are attached by substantial thongs. These trees are carefully and systematically trained, and they are trained so as to accomplish certain results. They present a large surface, in proportion to the whole, to the sun and air ; in addition to the direct rays of the sun, they receive the reflected and accumulated heat of the walls to which they are fastened ; and they furnish ripe fruit much in advance of trees in the gardens and fields of the common farmers. Here art and nature, in brick walls, manure, the germinating power of the peach or pear, and rigid training and pruning, have produced very good machines for the manufacture of fruit; but for the full-grown, symmetrically developed tree, or even for the choicest fruit in its season, we must look elsewhere. And who does not perceive, if all the trees of the gardens, fields, and forests, were treated in the same way, that the world would be deprived of a part of its beauty and glory, and that many species of trees would soon become extinct? Who would not give back the luscious pear and peach to their native acritude, rather than subject the highest forms of vegetable life to such irreverence? And, upon reflection, we shall say that such cruelty to inanimate life can be justified only as we justify the naturalist who dexterously and suddenly extracts a vital organ from a reptile, that he may observe the effect upon that form of animal existence.

But the tree is not to be left in its native state. By culture its growth is so aided, that it is first and always a tree after its own kind, whether it be peach, pear, apple, elm, or oak; at once ornamental and graceful, stately or majestic, according to the germinating principle which diffuses itself through each individual creation. "For the earth bringeth forth fruit of herself; first the blade, then the ear, after that the full corn in the ear." So in the human heart, mind, and soul, nature bringeth forth fruit of herself; and it is the work of schools and teachers to aid nature in developing a full and attractive character, that shall yield fruit while all its powers are enlarged and strengthened, as the almond in the peach is not only more luscious in its fruit, but more graceful in its branches. Culture, in a broad sense, is the aid rendered to each individual creation in its work of self-improvement. It is not a noble and generous culture which dwarfs the tree that early ripened or peculiarly flavored fruit may be obtained; and it is not a noble and generous culture of the child which forces into unnatural activity certain faculties or powers that surprise us by their precocity, or excite wonder by the skill exhibited in their use. Rather let the child grow, expand, mature, according to the law of its own being, giving it only encouragement and example, which are the light and air of mental and moral life. I am not conscious that any one has given us a philosophical, logical system of development, that relates to the physical, intellectual, and moral character; and to-day I state the educational want in this particular, but I do not attempt to supply it. Yet in nature such a system there must be, and only powers of observation are needed that we may avail ourselves of it. And in stating this want more particularly, I offer, as my first suggestion, the opinion, common among educators, that, speaking generally and with reference to a system, we have no physical training whatever.

In the days of our ancestors, one hundred or two hundred years ago, this training, as a part of a system of education, was not needed. We had no cities, and but few large towns. Agriculture and the ruder forms of mechanical labor were the chief occupations of the people. Populous cities, narrow streets, dark lanes, cellar habitations, crowded workshops, over-filled and over-heated factories, and the number of sedentary pursuits that tax and wear and destroy the physical powers, and undermine the moral and mental, were unknown. These are the attendants of our civilization, and they have brought a melancholy train of evils with them. In the seventeenth century, men perished from exposure, from ignorance of the laws of health, from the prevalence of malignant diseases that defied the science of the times; and, as a consequence, the average length of human life was not greater than it now is. At present, there is but little exposure that is followed by fatal results; malignant diseases are deprived of many of their terrors; rules of living, founded upon scientific principles, are accessible to all; and yet we daily meet young men and women who are manifestly unequal to the lot that is before them. In some cases, the sin of the parent is visited upon the children, and the measure of life meted out to them is limited and insufficient. In other cases, the individuals, first yielding in their own persons, are the victims of positive vice, or of some of the evils stated. Civilization is not an unmixed good; and we cannot offer to the city or the factory any adequate compensation for the loss of pure water, pure air, and the healthful exercise of body, which may be enjoyed in the country villages and agricultural districts of the state.

Yet even in cities and large towns the culture of home and school should diminish these evils; and it is a pleasure to believe that our system of domestic and public education is doing something at the present moment in behalf of the too much neglected body; but nowhere, either in city or country, do we observe the evidences of juvenile health and strength that a friend of the race would desire to see. And it is, I fear, specially true of schools, and to some extent it is true of teachers, as a class, that too little attention is given to those exercises and habits which secure good health. There are many causes which tend to lower the average health and strength of our people. 1st. The practice of sending children to school at the tender age of five, four, or even three years. Every school necessarily imposes some restraint upon the pupils; and I assume that no child under five years of age should be subject to such restraints. But the education of the child is not, therefore, to be neglected. Parents, brothers and sisters, may all do something for the young inquirer; but he should never have lessons imposed, nor be subject to the rules of a school of any description. The moment of his admission must be determined by circumstances, and the force of the circumstances must be judged of by parents. If a child is blessed with kind, considerate, intelligent parents, the first eight years of his life can be spent nowhere else as profitably as at home. The true mother is the model teacher. No other person can ever acquire the control over her offspring that is her own rightful possession. When she neglects the trust confided to her, she is guilty of a serious wrong; and when she transfers it to another, she takes upon herself a greater responsibility than she yields up. The instinctive judgment of the world cannot be an erroneous judgment. The mother has always, to a great extent, been made responsible for the child; and the honor of his virtues or the disgrace of his crimes has been traced through him to her.

2dly. Some portion of every school-day should be systematically and strictly devoted to recreation, physical exercise and manual labor; and the hours given to study ought to be defined and limited. Some persons say, "Let a child study as much as he will, there is time enough to play." This may be generally true, but it is not universally so. I cannot but think that the practice of assigning lessons and giving the pupil the free use of the four-and-twenty hours is a bad practice. Would it not be better to give to each pupil certain hours for study?—assign him lessons, by topics if possible, allow him to do what he can in the allotted time, and then prohibit the appropriation of an additional minute? Why should a dull scholar, or one who has but little taste or talent for a given study, be required to plod twelve, sixteen, or eighteen hours at unwelcome tasks, while another more favored disposes of his work in six? Why should a pupil, who is laboring under some mental or physical debility, be required to apply his mind unceasingly when he most needs rest and recreation? Why should the pages of a spelling-book, grammar, geography, or arithmetic, be the measure of each pupil's capacity? Lessons are to be assigned, not necessarily to be mastered by the pupil, though they should have just reference to his capacity, but as the subject of his studies for a given period of time. The pupil should be responsible for nothing but the proper use of that time. Two advantages might result from this practice.

First, the pupil would acquire the habit of performing the greatest amount of labor possible in the given time ; and, secondly, he would naturally throw off all care for books and school when the hour for relaxation arrived. If particular studies are assigned to specified hours, the pupil must master his thoughts, and give them the required direction. This in itself is a great achievement. I put it, in practical value, before any of the studies that are taught and learned in the schools. The danger to which pupils are often exposed, in this connection, is quite apparent. A lesson is assigned for a succeeding day. The attention is not immediately fixed upon it. One hour passes, and then another. Nothing is accomplished, yet the pupil is continually oppressed by the consciousness of duty unperformed, and the result is, that he neither does what he ought to do, nor does anything else. Would it not be better to measure and assign his time, and then require him to abandon all thought of the matter? This practice might give our people the faculty and the habit of throwing off cares and occupations, when they leave the scenes of them. It is a just criticism upon American character, that our business men carry their occupations with them wherever they go. I should put high up among the elements of worldly success the ability to give assiduously, studiously and devotedly, the necessary time to a subject of business, and then to throw off all thought of it. There can be no peace of mind for the business man who does not possess this quality; and I think it will contribute essentially to a long life and a quiet old age. No wise man ever attempts more than one thing at a time; and the man who attempts to do more than one thing at a time has no security that he can do anything well. The statements of biography and history, that Napoleon was accustomed to do several things at once, rest upon a misconception of the operations of the human mind. His facility for the direction and transaction of business depended upon the quality I am now considering. He had the faculty of giving his attention, undivided and strongly fixed, to a subject for an hour, half-hour, minute, half-minute, or second, and then of dismissing the matter altogether, and directing his thoughts, without loss of time, to whatever next might be presented. One thing at a time is a law which no finite power can violate; and ability in execution depends upon the ability to concentrate all the powers of the mind, at a given moment, upon the assigned topic, and then to change, without friction or loss of time, to something else.

This institution is a high school, and the question is now agitated, especially in the State of Connecticut, "How can the advantages of a high-school education be best secured?" This question I propose to consider. And, first, the high school must be a public school. A *public school* I understand to be a school established by the public, — supported chiefly or entirely by the public, controlled by the public, and accessible to the public upon terms of equality, without special charge for tuition.

Private schools may be established and controlled by an individual, or by an association of individuals, who have no corporate rights under the government, but receive pupils upon terms agreed upon, subject to the ordinary laws of the land.

Private schools may be founded also by one or more persons, and by them endowed with funds, for their partial or entire support. In such cases, the founder, through the money given, has the right to prescribe the rules by which the school shall be controlled, and also to provide for the appointment of its managers or trustees through all time. In such cases, corporate powers are usually granted by the government for the management of the business. But the chief rights of such an institution are derived from the founder, and the facilities for their easy exercise and quiet enjoyment are derived from the state.

Such schools are sometimes, upon a superficial view, supposed to be public, because they receive pupils upon terms of equality, and no rule of exclusion exists which does not apply to all. And especially has it been assumed that a free school thus founded, as the Norwich Free Academy, which makes no charges for tuition, and is open to all the inhabitants of the city, is therefore a public school. These institutions are public in their use, but not in their foundation or control, and are therefore not public schools. The character of a school, as of any eleemosynary institution, is derived from the will of the founder ; and when the beneficial founder is an individual, or a number of individuals less than the whole political organization of which the individuals are a part, the institution is private, whatever the rules for its enjoyment may be. To say that a school is a public school because it receives pupils free of charge for tuition, or because it receives them upon conditions that are applied alike to all, is to deny that there are any private schools, for all come within the definition thus laid down.

Nor is there any good reasoning in the statement that a school is public because it receives pupils from a large extent of country. Dartmouth College is a private school, though its pupils come from all the land or all the world ; while the Boston Latin School is a public school, though it receives those pupils only whose homes are within the limits of the city. The first is a private school, because it was founded by President Wheelock, and has been controlled by him and his successors, holding and governing and enjoying through him, from the first until now ; while the Boston Latin School is a public school, because it was established by the city of Boston, through the votes of its inhabitants, under the laws of the state, and is at all times subject, in its government and existence, to the popular will which created it. When we speak of the public we do not necessarily mean the world, nor the nation, nor even the state ; but the word *public,* in a legal sense, may stand for any legal political organization, territorially defined, and intrusted in any degree with the administration of its own affairs. And the public character of a particular school, as the Boston Latin School, for example, may be determined by a process of reasoning quite independent of that already presented. The State of Massachusetts, a complete sovereignty in itself, has provided by her constitution and laws, which are the expressed judgment of her people, for the establishment of a system of public schools, through the agency and action of the respective cities and towns of the commonwealth. These towns and cities, under the laws, set up the schools ; and of course each school partakes of the public character which the action of the state, followed by the corporate public action of the city or town, has given to it. Thus it is seen that our public schools answer to the requirement already stated. They are established by the public, supported chiefly or entirely by the public, controlled by the public, and accessible to the public upon terms of equality, without special charge for tuition. Nor is the public character of a school changed by the fact that private citizens may have contributed to its maintenance, if such contributors do not assume to stand in the relation of founders. It is well understood that the beneficial founder of a school is he who makes the first gift or bequest to it, and the legal founder is the government which grants a charter, or in any way confers upon it a corporate existence. If a town establish a high school, as in Bernardston to-day, and accept a gift or bequest, the character of the school is not changed thereby. Mr. Powers did not attempt to establish a new school. He gave the income of ten thousand dollars for the aid of schools then existing, and for the aid of a school whose existence was already contemplated by the laws of the state. No change has been wrought in your institutions; they are still public, — your generous testator has only contributed to their support. And, in considering yet further the question, "How can the advantages of a high-school education be best secured?" I shall proceed to compare, with what brevity I can command, the public high school with the free high school or academy upon a private foundation. My reasoning is general, and the argument does not apply to all the circumstances of society. It is not everywhere possible to establish a public high school. In some cases the population may not be sufficient, in others there may not be adequate wealth, and in others there may not be an elevated public sentiment equal to the emergency. In such circumstances, those who desire education must obtain it in the best manner possible; and academies, whether free or not, and private schools, whether endowed or not, should be thankfully accepted and encouraged. Nor will high schools meet all the wants of society. There must always be a place for classical schools, scientific schools, professional schools, which, in their respective courses of study, either anticipate or follow, in the career of the student, his four years of college life. With these conditions and limitations stated, the point I seek to establish is that a public high school can do the work usually done in such institutions more faithfully, thoroughly, and economically, than it can be done anywhere else.

1st. The supervision of the public school is more

responsible, and consequently more perfect. In private schools, academies and free high schools which are endowed, there is a board of trustees, who perpetuate, as a corporation, their own existence. Each member is elected for life, and he is not only not responsible to the public, but he is not even responsible, except in extraordinary cases, to his associates. Responsibility is, in all governments, the security taken for fidelity. The election of representatives, in the state or national legislature, for life, would be esteemed a great and dangerous innovation.

It may be said that boards of trustees are usually better qualified to manage a school than the committees elected by the respective cities and towns. Judged as individuals, this is probably true; though upon this point I prefer to admit a claim rather than to express an opinion. But positively incompetent school committees are the exception in Massachusetts; usually the people make the selection from their best men. But in the public school you get the immediate, direct supervision of the public. Not merely in the election of committees, but in a daily interest and vigilance whose results are freely disclosed to the superintending committee, as every inhabitant feels that his contribution, as a tax-payer, gives him the right to judge the character of the school, and makes it his duty to report its defects to those charged with its management. The real defects of a school, especially of a high school, will be first discovered by pupils; and they are likely to report these defects to their parents. In the case of the endowed private school, the parent feels that he buys whatever the trustees have to sell, or takes as a gift whatever they have to offer free; and he does not, logically nor as a matter of fact, infer from either of these relations his right to participate in the government of the school. In one case you have the observation, the judgment, the supervision, of the whole community; in the other case you have the learning and judgment of five, seven, ten, or twelve men.

2dly. The faithfulness of the teacher is very much dependent upon the supervision to which he is subject. This is only saying that the teacher is human. In the public school there is no motive which can influence a reasonable man that would lead him to swerve in the least from his fidelity to the interest of the school as a whole. No partiality to a particular individual, no desire to promulgate a special idea, can ever stand in the place of that public support which is best secured by a just performance of his duties. In the private school, with a self-perpetuating board of trustees, the temptation is strong to make the organization subservient to some opinion in politics, religion, or social life. This may not always be done; but in many cases it has been done, and there is no reason to expect different things in the future. I concur, then, unreservedly in the judgment which has placed this institution, in all its interests and in all its duties, under the control of the inhabitants of Bernardston. When they who live in its light and enjoy its benefits cease to respect it, when they to whom it is specially dedicated cease to love and cherish it, it will no longer be entitled to the favorable consideration of a more extended public sentiment. As all trustworthy national patriotism must be built on love for state, town, and home, so every school ought to esteem its power for usefulness in its own neighborhood its chief means of good.

It will naturally be inferred, from the remarks made upon the singleness of purpose and fidelity of the public school to the cause of education, that the instruction given in it is more thorough than is usually given in the private school. But, in examining yet further the claim of the public school to superior thoroughness, I must assume that it enjoys the advantages of comfortable rooms, adequate apparatus and competent teachers. And this assumption ought to be supported by the facts. There is no good reason why any town in Massachusetts should be negligent or parsimonious in these particulars. True economy requires liberal appropriations. With these appropriations, the best teachers, even from private schools and academies, can be secured, and all the aids and encouragements to liberal culture can be provided. Is it possible that any of the means of a common-school education are necessarily denied to a million and a quarter of industrious people, who already possess an aggregate capital of seven or eight hundred millions of dollars? But the character of a high school must always depend materially upon the previous training of the pupils, and the qualifications required for admission. When the high school is a public school, the studies of the primary and grammar or district schools are arranged with regard to the system as a system. There is no inducement to admit a pupil for the sake of the tuition fees, or for the purpose of adding to the number of scholars. The applicant is judged by his merits as a scholar; and where there is a wise public sentiment, the committee will be sustained in the execution of just rules.

In the public high school we avoid a difficulty that is almost universal in academies and private schools — the presence of pupils whose attainments are so various that by a proper classification they would be assigned to two, if not to three grades, where the graded system exists. The vigilance, industry and fidelity of teachers, cannot overcome this evil. The instruction given is inevitably less systematic and thorough. The character which the high school, whether public or private, presents, is not its own character merely; it reflects the qualities and peculiarities of the schools below. It follows, then, that the attention of the public should be as much directed to the primary and grammar or district schools as to the high school itself. Of course, it ought not to be assumed that the existence of a high school will warrant any abatement of appropriations for the lower grades; indeed, the interest and resources of these schools ought continually to increase.

Nor can it be assumed that your contributions to the cause of education will be diminished by the bequest of your generous testator. He did not seek to lessen your burdens, but to add to the means of education among you.

There is also an inherent power of discipline in the public schools, where they are graded and a system of examinations exists, that is not found elsewhere. Neither the pupil nor the parent is viewed by the teacher in the light of a patron; hence, he seeks only to so conduct his school as to meet the public requirement. Moreover, as admission to a high school can be secured by merit only, the results of the preliminary training must have been such as to create a reasonable presumption in favor of the applicant, mentally and morally. Hence, the public schools are filled by youth who are there as the reward of individual, personal merit. Practically, the motive by which the pupils are animated has much to do with their success. If they are moved by a love for learning, they attain the object of their desires even without the aid of teachers ; but where they are aided and encouraged by faithful teachers, the school is soon under the control of a public sentiment which secures the end in view.

This public sentiment is not as easily built up in a private school; for, in the nature of things, some pupils will find their way there who are not true disciples of learning; and such persons are obstacles to general progress, while they advance but little themselves.

And, gentlemen trustees and citizens of Bernardston, may I not personally and especially invite you to consider the importance of a fixed standard of admission and a careful examination of candidates? This course is essential to the improvement of your district and village schools. It is essential to the true prosperity of this seminary, and it is also essential to the intellectual advancement of the people within your influence. You expect pupils from the neighboring towns. Your object is not pecuniary profit, but the education of the people. If your requirements are positive, though it may not be difficult to meet them in the beginning, every town that depends upon this institution for better learning than it can furnish at home will be compelled to maintain schools of a high order. On the other hand, negligence in this particular will not only degrade the school under your care here, but the schools in this town and the cause of education in the vicinity will be unfavorably affected. Nor let the objection that a rigid standard of qualifications will exclude many pupils, and diminish the attendance upon the school, have great weight; for you perform but half your duty when you provide the means of a good education for your own students. You are also, through the power inherent in this authority, to do something to elevate the standard of learning in other schools, and in the country around. What harm if this school be small, while by its influence other schools are made better, and thus every boy and girl in the vicinity has richer means of education than could otherwise have been secured? Thus will tens, and hundreds, and thousands, of successive generations, have cause to bless this school, though they may never have sat under its teachers, or been within its walls.

In a system of public schools, everything may be had at its prime cost. There need be no waste of money, or of the time or power of teachers. As the public system must everywhere exist, it is a matter of economy to bring all the children under its influence. The private system never can educate all; therefore the public system cannot be abandoned, unless we consent to give up a part of the population to ignorance. It may, then, be said that the private schools, essential in many cases, ought to give way whenever the public schools are prepared to do the work; and when the public schools are so prepared, the existence of private schools adds their own cost to the necessary cost of popular education.

But we are not to encourage parsimony in education; for parsimony in this department is not true economy. It is true economy for the state and for a town to set up and maintain good schools as cheaply as they can be had, yet at any necessary cost, so only that they be good. Massachusetts is prosperous and wealthy to-day, respected in evil report as well as in good, because, faithful to principle and persistent in courage, she has for more than two hundred years provided for the education of her children; and now the re-flowing tide of her wealth from seaboard and cities will bear on its wave to these quiet valleys and pleasant hill-sides the lovers of agriculture, friends of art, students of science, and such as worship rural scenes and indulge in rural sports ; but the favored and first-sought spots will be those where learning has already chosen her seat, and offers to manhood and age the culture and society which learning only can give, and to childhood and youth, over and above the training of the best schools, healthful moral influences, and elements of physical growth and vigor, which ever distinguish life in the country and among the mountains from life in the city or on the plain. And over a broader field and upon a larger sphere shall the benignant influence of this system of public instruction be felt. In the affairs of this great republic, the power of a state is not to be measured by the number of its votes in Congress. Public opinion is mightier than Congress ; and they who wield or control that do, in reality, bear rule. Power in the world, upon a large view, and in the light of history, has not been confided to the majorities of men. Greece, unimportant in extent of territory, a peninsula and archipelago in the sea, led the way in the civilization of the west, and, through her eloquence, poetry, history and art, became the model of modern culture. Rome, a single city in Italy, that stretches itself into the sea as though it would gaze upon three continents, subjugated to her sway the savage and civilized world, and impressed her arms and jurisprudence upon all succeeding times; then Venice, without a single foot of solid land, guarded inviolate the treasure of her sovereignty for thirteen hundred years against the armies of the East and the West; while, in our own time, England, unimportant in the extent of her insular territory, has been able, by the intelligence and enterprise of her people, to make herself mistress of the seas, arbiter of the fortunes of Europe, and the ruler of a hundred millions of people in Asia.

These things have happened in obedience to a law which knows no change. Power in America is with those who can bring the greatest intellectual and moral force to bear upon a given point. And Massachusetts, limited in the extent of her territory, without salubrity of climate, fertility of soil, or wealth of mines, will have influence, through her people at home and her people abroad, proportionate to her fidelity to the cause of universal public education.

NORMAL SCHOOL TRAINING.

[An Address delivered at the Dedication of the State Normal School, at Salem.]

THE human race may be divided into two classes. One has no ideal of a future different from the present; or, if it is not always satisfied with this view, it has yet had no clear conception of a higher existence.

The other class is conscious of the power of progress, is making continual advances, and has an ideal of a future such as, in its judgment, the present ought to be. Both of these classes have institutions; for institutions are not the product of civilization, as they exist wherever our social nature is developed. Man is also a dependent being, and he therefore seeks the company, counsel and support of his fellows. From the right of numbers to act comes the necessity of agreement, or at least so much concurrence in what is to be done as to secure the object sought. The will of numbers can only be expressed through agencies; and these, however simple, are indeed institutions — the evidence of civilization, rather than its product. They are always the sign, symbol, or language, by which the living man expresses the purpose of his life. Therefore, institutions differ, as the purposes of men vary.

The savage and the man of culture do not seek the same end ; hence they will not employ the same means.

The institutions of the savage are those of the family, clan, or tribe, to which he belongs. There the child is instructed in the art of dress, in manners and language, in the rude customs of agriculture, the chase, and war. This with him is life, and the history of one generation is often the history of many generations. Their ideal corresponds with their actual life ; and, as a necessary result, there is little or no progress.

But the other class establishes institutions which indicate the existence of new relations, and exact the performance of new duties. As man is a social being, he necessarily creates institutions of government and education corresponding to the sphere in which he is to act. If a nation desires to educate only a part of its people, its institutions are naturally exclusive ; but wherever the idea of universal education has been received, the institutions of the country look to that end.

When Massachusetts was settled there were no truly popular institutions in the world, for there was really no belief in popular rights. And why should those be encouraged to think who have no right to act? The principle that every man is to take a part in the affairs of the community or state to which he belongs seems to be the foundation of the doctrine that every man should be educated to think for himself. Free schools and general education are the natural results of the principles of human equality, which distinguish the people and political systems of America.

The purposes of a people are changeable and changing, but institutions are inflexible; therefore these latter often outlast the ideas in which they originated, or the ideas may be acting in other bodies or forms. Institutions are the visible forms of ideas, but they are useful only while those ideas are living in the minds of men. If an institution is suffered to remain after the idea has passed away, it embarrasses rather than aids an advancing people. Such are monastic establishments in Protestant countries; such is the Church of England, as an institution of religion and government, to all classes of dissenters; such are many seminaries of learning in Europe, and some in America.

Massachusetts has had one living idea, from the first, — that general intelligence is necessary to popular virtue and liberty. This idea she has expressed in various ways; the end it promises she has sought by various means. In obedience to this idea, she has established colleges, common schools, grammar schools, academies, and at last the Normal School.

The *institution* only of the Normal School is new; the *idea* is old. The Normal system is but a better expression of an idea partially concealed, but nevertheless to be found in the college, grammar school and academy of our fathers. Nor have we accepted the institution so readily from a knowledge of its results in other countries, as from its manifest fitness to meet a want here. It is not, then, our fortune to inaugurate a new idea, but only to clothe an old one again, so that it may more efficiently advance popular liberty, intelligence and virtue. And this is our duty to-day.

The proprieties of this occasion would have been better observed, had his excellency, Governor Washburn, found it convenient to deliver the address, which, at a late moment, has been assigned to me. But we are all in some degree aware of the nature and extent of his public duties, and can, therefore, appreciate the necessity which demands relief from some of them.

Massachusetts has founded four Normal Schools, and at the close of the present century she may not have established as many more, for she now satisfies the just demands of every section of her territory, and presents the benefits of this system of instruction to all her inhabitants. The building we here set apart, and the school we now inaugurate to the service of learning, are to be regarded as the completion of the original plan of the state, and any future extension will depend upon the success of the Normal system as it shall appear in other years to other generations of men. But we have great faith that the Normal system, in itself and in its connections, will realize the cherished idea of our whole history; and if so, it will be extended until every school is supplied with a Normal teacher.

This, then, is an occasion of general interest; but to the city of Salem, and the county of Essex, it is specially important. Similar institutions have been long established in other parts of the state; but some compensation is now to be made to you, in the experience and improvements of the last fifteen years. Intelligent labor sheds light upon the path of the laborer, and, though the direct benefits of this system have not been here enjoyed, many resulting advantages from the experience of similar institutions in other places will now inure to you.

The city of Salem, with wise forecast, anticipated these advantages, and generously contributed a sum larger even than that appropriated by the state itself. This bounty determined the location of the school, but determined it fortunately for all concerned.

Salem is one of the central points of the state; and in this respect no other town in the vicinity, however well situated, is a competitor. Pupils may reside at their homes in Newburyport, Lynn, Lawrence, Haverhill, Gloucester and Lowell, or at any intermediate place, and enjoy the benefit of daily instruction within these walls. This is a great privilege for parents and pupils; and it could not have been so well secured at any other point. Here, also, pupils and teachers may avail themselves of the libraries, literary institutions and cabinets of this ancient and prosperous town. These are no common advantages.

We are wiser and better for the presence of great numbers of books, though we may never know what they contain. We see how much perseverance and labor have accomplished, and are sensible that what has been may be equalled if not excelled. In great libraries, we realize how the works of the ambitious are neglected, and their names forgotten, while we cannot fail to be impressed with the value of the truth, that the only labor which brings a certain reward is that performed under a sense of duty.

Salem is itself the intelligent and refined centre of an intelligent and prosperous population; and we may venture so far, in just eulogy, as to attribute to it the united advantages of city and country, without a large share of the privations of the one, or the vices of the other. Of the four Normal Schools, this is, unquestionably, the most fortunate in its position and surroundings. We, therefore, ask for the concurrence of the public in the judgment which has established it in this city. If it shall be the fortune of the government to assemble a body of instructors qualified for their stations, there will then remain no reason why these accommodations and advantages should not be fully enjoyed.

The Normal School differs from all other seminaries of learning, and only because it is an auxiliary to the common schools can it be deemed their inferior in importance. The academy and college take young men from the district and high schools, and furnish them with additional aids for the business of life; but the Normal School is truly the helper of the common schools. It receives its pupils from them, fits these pupils for teachers, and sends them back to superintend where a few months before they were scholars. The Normal Schools are sustained by the common schools; and these latter, in return, draw their best nutriment from the former. This institution stands with the common school; it is as truly popular, as really democratic in a just sense, and its claim for support rests upon the same foundation.

In Massachusetts we have abandoned the idea, never, I think, general, that instruction in the art of teaching is unnecessary.

The Normal School is, with us, a necessity; for it furnishes that tuition which neither the common school, academy, nor college can. These institutions were once better adapted to this service than now. There has been a continual increase of academic studies, until it has become necessary to establish institutions for special purposes; and of these the Normal School is one. Its object is definite. The *true* Normal School instructs only in the art of teaching; and, in this respect, it must be confessed we have failed, sadly failed, to realize the ideal of the system. It is not a substitute for the common school, academy, or college, though many pupils, and in some degree the public, have been inclined thus to treat it. There should be no instruction in the departments of learning, high or low, except what is incidental to the main business of the institution; yet some have gone so far in the wrong course as to suggest that not only the common branchės should be studied, but that tuition should be given in the languages and the higher mathematics. A little reflection will satisfy us how great a departure this would be from the just idea of the Normal School. Yet circumstances, rather than public sentiment, have compelled the government to depart in practice, though never in theory, from the true system.

It so happens that much time is occupied in instruction in those branches which ought to be thoroughly mastered by the pupil before he enters the Normal School,—that is, before he begins to acquire the art of teaching what he has not himself learned.

Such is the state of our schools that we are obliged to accept as pupils those who are not qualified, in a literary point of view, for the post of teachers. By sending better teachers into the public schools, you will effectually aid in the removal of this difficulty. The Normal School is, then, no substitute for the high school, academy, or college. Nor do we ask for any sympathy or aid which properly belongs to those institutions. He is no friend of education, in its proper signification, who patronizes some one institution, and neglects all others. We have no seminaries of learning which can be considered useless, and he only is a true friend who aids and encourages any and all as he has opportunity. What is popularly known as learning is to be acquired in the common school, high school, academy and college, as heretofore. The Normal School does not profess to give instruction in reading and arithmetic, but to teach the art of teaching reading and arithmetic. So of all the elementary branches. But, as the art of teaching a subject cannot be acquired without at the same time acquiring a better knowledge of the subject itself, the pupil will always leave the Normal School better grounded than ever before in the elements and principles of learning. It is not, however, to be expected that complete success will be realized here more than elsewhere ; yet it is well to elevate the standard of admission, from time to time, so that a larger part of the exercises may be devoted to the main purpose of the institution. The struggle should be perpetual and in the right direction. First, elevate your common schools so that the education there may be a sufficient basis for a course of training here. If the Normal School and the public schools shall each and all do their duty, candidates for admission will be so well qualified in the branches required, that the art of teaching will be the only art taught here. When this is the case, the time of attendance will be diminished, and a much larger number of persons may be annually qualified for the station of teachers.

Next, let the committees and others interested in

education make special efforts to fill the chairs of your hall with young women of promise, who are likely to devote themselves to the profession. It is, however, impossible for human wisdom to guard against one fate that happens to all, or nearly all, the young women who are graduated at our Normal Schools. But this remark is not made publicly, lest some anxious ones avail themselves of your bounty as a means to an end not contemplated by the state.

The house you have erected is not so much dedicated to the school as to the public ; the institution here set up is not so much for the benefit of the young women who may become pupils, as for the benefit of the public which they represent. The appeal is, therefore, to the public to furnish such pupils, in number and character, that this institution may soon and successfully enter upon the work for which it is properly designed.

But the character and value of this school depend on the quality of its teachers more than on all things else. They should be thoroughly instructed, not only in the branches taught, but in the art of teaching them.

The teacher ought to have attained much that the pupil is yet to learn ; if he has not, he cannot utter words of encouragement, nor estimate the chances of success. It is not enough to know what is contained in the text-book ; the pupil should know that, at least ; the teacher should know a great deal more. A person is not qualified for the office of teacher when he has mastered a book ; and has, in fact, no right to instruct others until he has mastered the subject.

Text-books help us a little on the road of learning ; but, by and by, whatever our pursuit or profession, we leave them behind, or else content ourselves with a subordinate position. Practical men have made book-farmers the subject of ridicule ; and there is some propriety in this ; for he is not a master in his profession who has not got, as a general thing, out of and beyond the books which treat of it.

Books are necessary in the school-room ; but the good teacher has little use for them in his own hands, or as aids in his own proper work. He should be instructed in his subject, aside from and above the arbitrary rules of authors ; and he will be, if he is himself inspired with a love of learning. *Inspired with a love of learning!* Whoever is, is sure of success ; and whoever is not, has the best possible security for the failure of his plans. There cannot be a good school where the love of learning in teacher and pupil is wanting ; and there cannot be a bad one where this spirit has control. As the master, so is the disciple ; as the teacher, so is the pupil; for the spirit of the teacher will be communicated to the scholars. There must also be habits of industry and system in study. We have multitudes of scholars who study occasionally, and study hard; but we need a race of students who will devote themselves habitually, and with love, to literature and science.

On the teachers, then, is the chief responsibility, whether the young women who go out from this institution are well qualified for their profession or not. The study of technicalities is drudgery of the worst sort to the mere pupil; but the scholar looks upon it as a preparation for a wide and noble exercise of his intellectual powers — as a key to unlock the mysteries of learning. It is the business of the teacher to lighten the labors of to-day by bright visions of to-morrow.

There is a school in medicine, whose chief claim is, that it invites and prepares Nature to act in the removal of disease.

We pass no judgment upon this claim; but he is, no doubt, the best teacher who does little for his pupils, while he incites and encourages them to do much for themselves. Extensive knowledge will enable the teacher to do this.

He is a poor instructor of mathematics who sees only the dry details of rules, tables and problems, and never ascends to the contemplation of those supreme wonders of the universe which mathematical astronomy has laid open. The grammar of a language is defined to be the art of reading and writing that language with propriety. The study of its elements is dry and uninteresting ; and, while the teacher dwells with care upon the merits of the text, he should also lift the veil from that which is hidden, and lead his pupils to appreciate those riches of learning which the knowledge of a language may confer upon the student.

It is useful to know the division of the globe into continents and oceans, islands and lakes, mountains and rivers — and this knowledge the text-books contain ; but it is a higher learning to understand the effect of this division upon climate, soil and natural productions — upon the character and pursuits of the human race. Books are so improved that they may very well take the place of poor, or even ordinary teachers.

Explanations and illustrations are numerous and appropriate, and very little remains for the mere text-book teacher to do. But, when the duties of teacher and the exercises of the school-room are properly performed, the entire range of science, business, literature and art, is presented to the student. May it be your fortune to see education thus elevated here, and then will the same spirit be infused into the public schools of the vicinity.

The Massachusetts system of education is a noble tribute to freedom of thought. The power of educating a people, which is, in fine, the chief power in a state, has been often, if not usually, perverted to the support of favored opinions in religion and government. The boasted system of Prussia is only a prop and ally of the existing order of things. In France, Napoleon makes the press, which has become in civilized countries an educator of the people, the mere instrument of his will. Tyrants do not hesitate to pervert schools and the press, learning and literature, to the support of tyranny. But with us the press and the school are free ; and this freedom, denied through fear in other countries, is the best evidence of the stability of our institutions. It is now a hundred years since an attempt was made in Massachusetts to exercise legal censorship over the press ; but we occasionally hear of movements to make the public schools of America subservient to sect or party. The success of these movements would be as great a calamity as can ever befall a free people. Ignorance would take the place of learning, and slavery would usurp the domain of liberty.

No defence, excuse, or palliation, can be offered

for such movements; and their triumph will surely produce all the evils which it is possible for an enlightened people to endure. Our system of instruction is what it professes to be, — a public system. As sects or parties, we have no claim whatever upon it. A man is not taxed because he is of a particular faith in religion, or party in politics; he is not taxed because he is the father of a family, or excused because he is not; but he contributes to the cause of education because he is a citizen, and has an interest in that general intelligence which decides questions of faith and practice as they arise. It is for the interest of all that all shall be educated for the various pursuits and duties of the time. The education of children is, no doubt, first in individual duty. It is the duty of the parent, the duty of the friend; but, above all, it is the duty of the public. This duty arises from the relations of men in every civilized state; but in a popular government it becomes a necessity. The people are the source of power — the sovereign. And is it more important in a monarchy than in a republic that the ruler be intelligent, virtuous, and in all respects qualified for his duties?

The institution here set up is an essential part of our system of public instruction, and, as such, it claims the public favor, sympathy and support.

This is a period of excitement in all the affairs and

relations of men, and America is fast becoming the central point of these activities. They are, no doubt, associated with many blessings, but they may also be attended by great evils. We claim for our country preëminence in education. This may be just, but it is also true that Americans, more than any other people, need to be better educated than they are. Where else is the field of statesmanship so large, or the necessity for able statesmen so great?

With the single exception of Great Britain, there is no nation whose relations are such as to require a union in rulers of the rarest practical abilities with accurate, sound and varied learning; and there is no nation whose people are so critical in the tests they apply to their public agents. We need men thoroughly educated in all the departments of learning; to which ought to be added, travel in foreign countries, and an intimate acquaintance with every part of our own. Such men we have had — such men we have now; but they will be more and more important as we advance in numbers, territory and power. A corresponding culture is necessary in theology, in law, and in all the pursuits of industry.

No other nation has so great a destiny. That destiny is manifest, and may be read in the heart and purpose of the people. They seek new territories, an increase of population, the prosperity of commerce, of all the arts of industry, and preëminence in virtue, learning and intellectual power. And all this they can attain ; for the destiny of a people, within the limits prescribed by reason, is determined by themselves. If, however, by conquest, annexation and absorption, we acquire new territories, and strange races and nations of men, and yet neglect education, every step will but increase our burdens and perils, and hasten our decay.

FEMALE EDUCATION.

[An Address before the Newburyport Female High School.]

I ACCEPTED, without a moment's delay, the invitation of the principal of this school to deliver the customary address on this, the fifteenth anniversary of its establishment. My presence here in connection with public instruction is not a proper subject for comment by myself; but I have now come, allow me to say, with unusual alacrity, that we may together recognize the claims of an institution which furnishes the earliest evidence existing among us of a special design on the part of the public to provide adequate intellectual and moral training for the young women of the state.

Those movements which have accomplished most for religion, liberty, and learning, have not been sudden in their origin nor rapid in their progress. Christianity has been preached eighteen hundred years, yet it is not now received, even intellectually, by the larger part of the human race. Magna Charta is six centuries old, but its principles are not accepted by all the nations of Europe and America;

and it is not, therefore, strange that a system of public instruction, originated by the Puritans of New England, should yet be struggling against prejudice and error. In Asia woman is degraded, and in Europe her common condition is that of apparent and absolute inferiority. When America was settled she became a participator in the struggles and sufferings which awaited the pioneers of civilization and liberty on this continent, and she thus earned a place in family, religious, and even in public life, which foreshowed her certain and speedy disenthrallment from the tyranny of tradition and time. Her rights with us are secure, and the anxiety and boisterous alarm exhibited by some strong-minded women, and the horror-fringed apprehensions and prophecies of some weak-minded men, are equally unreasonable and absurd. Woman is sharing the lot of humanity, and therewith she ought to be content. Man does not remove the burden of ignorance and oppression from his sex, merely, but generally from his kind. At least, this is the experience and promise of America. If woman does not vote because she is woman, so and for the same reason she is not subject to personal taxation. It is an error to suppose that voting is a privilege, and taxation, ever and always, a burden. Both are duties; and the privilege of the one and the burden of the other are only incidental and subordinate. The human family is an aggregation of families; and the family, not the man nor the woman, is the unit of the state. The civil law assumes the existence of the family relation, and its unity where it exists; hence taxation of the woman brings no revenue to the state that might not have been secured by the taxation of the man; and hence the exercise of the elective franchise by the woman brings no additional political power; for, in the theory of the relation to which there are, in fact, but few exceptions, there is in the household but one political idea, and but one agent is needed for its expression. The ballot is the judgment of the family; not of the man, merely, nor of the woman, nor yet, indeed, always of both, even. The first smile that the father receives from the child affects every subsequent vote in municipal concerns, and likely enough also in national affairs. From that moment forward, he judges constables, selectmen, magistrates, aldermen, mayors, school-committees, and councillors, with an altered judgment. The result of the election is not the victory or defeat of the man alone; it is the triumph or prostration of a principle or purpose with which the family is identified.

Is it said that there is occasionally, if not frequently, a divided judgment in the household upon those questions that are decided by the ballot? This must, of course, be granted as an exceptional condition of domestic life ; but, for the wisest reasons of public policy, whose avoidance by the state would be treachery to humanity, the law universal can recognize only the general condition of things. So, and for kindred but not equally strong reasons, the elective franchise is exercised by men without families, and denied to those women who by the dispensations of Divine Providence are called to preside in homes where the father's face is seen no more. But why, in the eye of the state, shall the man stand as the head of the family, rather than the woman ? Because God has so ordained it ; and no civil community has ever yet escaped from the force of His decree in this respect. Those whose physical power defends the nation, or tribe, or family, are naturally called upon to decide what the means of defence shall be. Is not woman, then, the equal of man ? We cannot say of woman, with reference to man, that she is his superior, or his inferior, or his equal ; nor can we say of man, with reference to woman, that he is her superior, or her inferior, or her equal. He is her protector, she is his helpmeet. His strength is sufficient for her weakness, and her power is the support of his irresolution and want of faith. Woman's rights are not man's rights ; nor are man's rights the measure of woman's rights. If she should assert her independence, as some idiosyncratic persons desire, she could only declare her intention to do all those acts and things which woman may of right do. Given that this is accomplished, and I know not that she would possess one additional domestic, political, or public right, or enjoy one privilege in the family, neighborhood, or state, to which she is not, in some degree, at least, already accustomed.

These views and reflections may serve to illustrate and enforce the leading position of this address — that we are to educate young women for the enjoyments and duties of the sphere in which they are to move. We speak to-day of public instruction ; but it should ever be borne in mind that the education of the schools is but a part, and often only the least important part, of the training that the young receive. There is the training of infancy and early childhood, the daily culture of home, with its refining or deadening influences, and then the education of the street, the parlor, the festive gathering, and the clubs, which exert a power over the youth of both sexes that cannot often be controlled entirely by the school.

Womanhood is sometimes sacrificed in childhood, when the mother and the family fail to develop the womanly qualities of modesty, grace, generosity of character, and geniality of temper, which dignify, adorn, and protect,

> "The sex whose presence civilizes ours."

The child, whether girl or boy, reflects the character of its home; and therefore we are compelled to deal with all the homes of the district or town, and are required often to counteract the influences they exert. Early vicious training is quite as disastrous to the girl as to the boy; for, strange as it may seem, the world more readily tolerates ignorance, coarseness, rudeness, immodesty, and all their answering vices, in man than in woman. In the period of life from eight to twenty years of age the progress of woman is, to us of sterner mould, inconceivably rapid; but from twenty to forty the advantages of education are upon the other side. It then follows that a defective system of education is more pernicious to woman than to man.

We may contemplate woman in four relations with their answering responsibilities — as pupil, teacher, companion, and mother. As a pupil, she is sensitive, conscientious, quick, ambitious, and possesses in a marvellous degree, as compared with the other sex, the power of intuition. The boy is logical, or he is nothing; but logic is not necessary for the girl. Not that she is illogical; but she usually sees through, without observing the steps in the process which a boy must discern before he can comprehend the subject presented to his mind. In the use of the eye, the ear, the voice, and in the appropriation of whatever may be commanded without the highest exercise of the reasoning and reflective faculties, she is incomparably superior. She accepts moral truth without waiting for a demonstration, and she obeys the law founded upon it without being its slave. She instinctively prefers good manners to faulty habits; and, in the requirements of family, social, and fashionable life, she is better educated at sixteen than her brother is at twenty. She is an adept in one only of the vices of the school — whispering — and in that she excels. But she does not so readily resort to the great vice — the crime of falsehood — as do her companions of the other sex. I call falsehood the great vice, because, if this were unknown, tardiness, truancy, obscenity, and profanity, could not thrive. Holmes has well said that "sin has many tools, but a lie is the handle that will fit them all."

In many primary and district schools the habits and manners of children are too much neglected. We associate good habits and good manners with good morals; and, though we are deceived again and again, and soliloquize upon the maxim that "all is not gold that glitters," we instinctively believe, however often we are betrayed. Habits and manners are the first evidence of character; and so much of weight do we attach to such evidence, that we give credit and confidence to those whom in our calmer moments we know to be unworthy. The first aim in the school should be to build up a character that shall be truthfully indicated by purity and refinement of manner and conversation. It does, indeed, sometimes happen that purity of character is not associated with refinement of manners. This misfortune is traceable to a defective early education, both in the school and the home; for, had either been faithful and intelligent, the evil would have been averted. And, as there are many homes in city and country where refinement of manners is not found, and, of course, cannot be taught, the schools must furnish the training. In this connection, the value of the high school for females—whether exclusively so or not, does not seem to me important—is clearly seen. Young women are naturally and properly the teachers of primary, district, and subordinate schools of every grade; and society as naturally and properly looks to them to educate, by example as well as by precept, all the children of the state in good habits, good manners, and good morals. We are also permitted to look forward to the higher relations of life, when, as wives and mothers, they are to exert a potent influence over existing and future generations. The law and the lexicons say "*home* is the house or the place where one resides." This definition may answer for the law and the lexicons, but it does not meet the wants of common life.

The wife will usually find in her husband less refinement of manners than she herself possesses; and it is her great privilege, if not her solemn duty, to illustrate the line of Cowper, and show that she is of

"The sex whose presence civilizes ours."

It is the duty of the teacher to make the school attractive; and what the teacher should do for the school the wife should do for the home. The home should be preferred by the husband and children to all other places. Much depends upon themselves; they have no right to claim all of the wife and mother. But, without her aid, they can do but little. With her aid, every desirable result may be accomplished. That this result may be secured, female education must be generous, critical, and pure, in everything that relates to manners, habits, and morals. Much may be added to these, but nothing can serve in their stead. We should add, no doubt, thorough elementary training in reading, writing, and spelling, both for her own good and for the service of her children. Intellectual training is defective where these elements aré neglected, and their importance to the sexes may be equal. We should not omit music and the culture of the voice. The tones of the voice indicate the tone of the mind; but the temper itself may finally yield to a graceful and gentle form of expression. It is not probable that we shall ever give due attention to the cultivation of the human voice for speaking, reading, and singing. This is an invaluable accomplishment in man. Many of us have listened to New England's most distinguished living orator, and felt that well-known lines from the English poets derived new power, if not actual inspiration, from the classic tones in which the words were uttered.

A cultivated voice in woman is at once the evidence and the means of moral power. As the moral sensibilities of the girl are more acute than those of the boy, so the moral power of the woman is greater than that of the man. Many young women are educating themselves for the business of teaching; and I can commend nothing more important, after the proper ordering of one's own life, than the discreet and careful training of the voice. It is itself a power. It demands sympathy before the suffering or its cause is revealed by articulate speech; its tones awe assemblies, and command silence before the speaker announces his views ; and the rebellious and disorderly, whether in the school, around the rostrum, or on the field, bow in submission beneath the authority of its majestic cadences. It is hardly possible to imagine a good school, and very rare to see one, where this power is wanting in the teacher. Women are often called to take charge of schools where there are lads and youth destitute of that culture which would lead them to yield respect and consequent obedience. Physical force in these cases is not usually to be thought of; but nature has vouchsafed to woman such a degree of moral power, of which in the school the voice is the best expression, as often to fully compensate for her weakness in other respects.

It is unnecessary to commend reading as an art and an accomplishment; but good readers are so rare among us, that we cannot too strongly urge teachers to qualify themselves for the great work. I say *great work,* because everything else is comparatively easy to the teacher, and comparatively unimportant to the pupil. Grammar is merely an element of reading. It should be introduced as soon as the child's reasoning faculties are in any degree developed, and presented by the living voice, without the aid of books. The alphabet should be taught in connection with exercises for strengthening and modulating the voice, and the elementary sounds of the letters should be deemed as important as their names. All this is the proper work of the female teacher; and, when she is ignorant or neglects her duty, the evil is usually so great as to admit of no complete remedy.

Reading is at once an imitative and an appreciative art on the part of the pupil. He must be trained to appreciate the meaning of the writer; but he will depend upon the teacher at first, and, indeed, for a long time, for an example of the true mode of expression. This the teacher must be ready to give. It is not enough that she can correct faults of pronunciation, censure inarticulate utterances, and condemn gruff, nasal, and guttural sounds; but she must be able to present, in reasonable purity, all the opposite qualities. The young women have not yet done their duty to the cause of education in these respects; nor is there everywhere a public sentiment that will even now allow the duty to be performed.

It is difficult to see why the child of five, and the youth of fifteen, should be kept an equal number of hours at school. Each pupil should spend as much time in the school-room as is needed for the preparation of the exercise and the exercise itself. The danger from excessive confinement and labor is with young pupils. Those in grammar and high schools may often use additional hours for study; but a pupil should be somewhat advanced, and should possess considerable physical strength and endurance, before he ventures to give more than six hours a day to severe intellectual labor. It must often happen that children in primary schools can learn in two hours each day all that the teacher has time to communicate, or they have power to receive and appropriate. Indeed, I think this is usually so. It may not, however, be safe to deduce from this fact the opinion that children should never be kept longer in school than two hours a day; but it seems proper to assume that, if blessed with good homes, they may be relieved from the tedium of confinement in the school-room, when there is no longer opportunity for improvement.

We are beginning to realize the advantages of well-educated female teachers in primary schools; nor do I deem it improbable that they shall become successful teachers and managers of schools of higher grade, according to the present public estimation. But, in regard to the latter position, I have neither hope, desire, nor anxiety. Whenever the public judge them, generally, or in particular cases, qualified to take charge of high schools and normal schools, those positions will be assigned to them; and, till that degree of public confidence is accorded, it is useless to make assertions or indulge in conjectures concerning the ability of women for such duties. It is my own conviction that a higher order of teaching talent is required in the primary school, or for the early, judicious education of children, than is required in any other institutions of learning. Nor can it be shown that equal ability for government is not essential. There must be different manifestations of ability in the primary and the high school; but, where proper training has been enjoyed, pupils in the latter ought to be far advanced in the acquisition of the cardinal virtue of self-control, whose existence in the school and the state renders government comparatively unnecessary.

Where there is a human being, there are the opportunity and the duty of education. But our present great concern, as friends of learning, is with those schools where children are first trained in the elements. If in these we can have faithful, accurate, systematic, comprehensive teaching, everything else desirable will be added thereunto. But, if we are negligent, unphilosophical, and false, the reasonable public expectation will never be realized in regard to other institutions of learning.

The work must be done by women, and by well-educated women; and, when it is said that in Massachusetts alone we need the services of six thousand such persons, the magnitude of the work of providing teachers may be appreciated. Have we not enough in this field for every female school and academy, where high schools are not required, or cannot exist, and for every high school and normal school in the commonwealth? If it is asserted that the supply of female teachers is already greater than the demand, it must be stated, in reply, that there are persons enough engaged in teaching, but that the number of competent teachers is, and ever has been, too small. It is something, my friends, it is often a great deal, to send into a town a well-qualified female teacher. She is not only a blessing to those who are under her tuition, but her example and influence are often such as to change the local sentiment concerning teachers and schools. When may we expect a supply of such persons? The hope is not a delusion, though its realization may be many years postponed. How are competent persons to be selected and qualified? The change will be gradual, and it is to be made in the public opinion as well as in the character of teachers and schools. And is it not possible, even in view of all that has been accomplished, that we are yet groping in a dark passage, with only the hope that it leads to an outward-opening door, where, in marvellous but genial light, we shall perceive new truths concerning the philosophy of the human mind, and the means of its development? At this moment we are compelled to admit that practical teachers and theorists in educational matters are alike uncertain in regard to the true method of teaching the alphabet, and divided and subdivided in opinion concerning the order of succession of the various studies in the primary and grammar schools. Perfect agreement on these points is not probable; it may not be desirable. I am satisfied that no greater contribution can be made to the cause of learning than a presentation of these topics and their elucidation, so that the teacher shall feel that what he does is philosophical, and therefore wise.

The only way to achieve success is to apply faithfully the means at hand. Generations of children cannot wait for perfection in methods of teaching; but teachers of primary schools ought not to neglect any opportunity which promises aid to them as individuals, or progress in the profession that they have chosen. As teachers improve, so do schools; and, as schools improve, so do teachers. The influence exerted by teachers is first beneficial to pupils, but, as a result, we soon have a class of better qualified teachers. With these ideas of the importance of the teacher's vocation to primary instruction, and, consequently, to all good learning, it is not strange that I place a high value upon professional training. A degree of professional training more or less desirable is, no doubt, furnished by every school; but the admission does not in any manner detract from the force of the statement that a young man or woman well qualified in the branches to be taught, yet without experience, may be strengthened and prepared for the work of teaching, by devoting six, twelve, or eighteen months, under competent instructors, in company with a hundred other persons having a similar object in view, to the study, examination, and discussion, of those subjects and topics which are sometimes connected with, and sometimes independent of, the text-books, but which are of daily value to the teacher.

At present only a portion of this necessary professional training can be given in the normal schools. If, however, as I trust may sometimes be the case, none should be admitted but those who are already qualified in the branches to be taught, the time of attendance might be diminished, and the number of graduates proportionately increased. There are about one hundred high schools in the state, and, within the sphere of their labors, they are not equalled by any institutions that the world has seen. Young men are fitted for the colleges, for mechanical, manufacturing, commercial, agricultural, and scientific labors, and young men and young women are prepared for the general duties of life. They are also furnishing a large number of well-qualified teachers. Some may say that with these results we ought to be content. Regarding only the past, they are entirely satisfactory; but, animated with reasonable hopes concerning the future, we claim something more and better. It is not disguised that the members of normal schools, when admitted, do not sustain an average rank in scholarship with graduates of high schools. This is a misfortune from which relief is sought. It is a suggestion, diffidently made, yet with considerable confidence in its practicability and value, that graduates of high schools will often obtain additional and necessary preparation by attending a normal school, if for the term of six months only. And I am satisfied, beyond all reasonable doubt, that, when the normal schools receive only those whose education is equivalent to that now given in the high schools, a body of teachers will be sent out who will surpass the graduates of any other institution, and whose average professional attainments and practical excellence will meet the highest reasonable public expectation. Nor is it claimed that this result will be due to anything known or practised in normal schools that may not be known and practised elsewhere; but it is rather attributable to the fact that in these institutions the attention of teachers and pupils is directed almost exclusively to the work of teaching, and the means of preparation. The studies, thoughts, and discussions, are devoted to this end. If, with such opportunities, there should be no progress, we should be led to doubt all our previous knowledge of human character, and of the development of the youthful mind.

And now, ladies and gentlemen, before I conclude, allow me to remove, or at least to lessen, an impression that these remarks are calculated to produce. I have assumed that teaching is a profession — an arduous profession — and that perfection has not yet been attained. I have assumed, also, that there are many persons engaged in teaching, especially in the primary and mixed district schools, whose qualifications are not as great as they ought to be. But let it not be thence inferred that I am dissatisfied with our teachers and schools. There has been continual progress in education, and a large share of this progress is due to teachers; but the time has not yet come when we can wisely fold our arms, and accept the allurements of undisturbed repose.

Nor have I sought, on this occasion, to present even an outline of a system of female education. In all the public institutions of learning among us, it should be as comprehensive, as minute, as exact, as that furnished for youth of the other sex. Nor is it necessary to concern ourselves about the effect of this liberal culture upon the character and fortunes of society. I do not anticipate any sudden or disastrous effects. The right of education is a common right; and it is unquestionably the right of woman to assert her rights; and it is a wrong and sin if we withhold any, even the least. Having faith in humanity, and faith in God, let us not shrink from the privilege we enjoy of offering to all, without reference to sex or condition, the benefits of a public and liberal system of education, which seeks, in an alliance with virtue and religion, whose banns are forbidden by none, to enlighten the ignorant, restrain and reform the depraved, and penetrate all society with good learning and civilization, so that the highest idea of a well-ordered state shall be realized in an advanced and advancing condition of individual and family life.

THE INFLUENCE, DUTIES, AND REWARDS, OF TEACHERS.

[A Lecture delivered at Teachers' Institutes.]

It is the purpose, and we believe that it will be the destiny, of Massachusetts, to build up a comparatively perfect system of public instruction. To this antiquity did not aspire; and it is the just boast of modern times, and especially of the American States, that learning is not the amusement of a few only, whom wealth and taste have led into its paths, but that it is encouraged by governments, and cherished by the whole people. Antiquity had its schools and teachers; but the latter were, for the most part, founders of sects in politics, morals, philosophy, religion, or the habits of daily life; while its schools were frequented and sustained by those who sought to build on the civilization of the times such structures as their tastes conceived or their opinions dictated.

There were not in Athens or Rome, according to the American idea, any schools for the people; and Carlyle, Brownson, and Emerson, are such teachers in kind, though not in power and influence, as were Socrates, Plato, and Aristotle. These men were leaders as well as teachers, and their followers were disciples and controversialists rather than pupils. But it is not possible for modern leaders in politics, philosophy, and social life, to rival the ancients. Manual labor is not more divided and subdivided than is the influence of the human intellect. The newspaper has inspired every man with the love of self-judgment, and the common school has qualified him, in some degree, for its exercise. The ancients, whose names and fame have come down to us, taught by conversations, discussions, and lectures; the moderns, as Carlyle, Brownson, and Emerson, by lectures, essays, and reviews. But these systems are quite inadequate to meet the wants of American civilization.

Indeed, however men of talent may strive, there cannot be another Socrates, Plato, or Aristotle; for the printing-press has come, and their occupation has gone. Teachers were philosophers, pupils were followers and disciples, while learning was devoted to the support of speculations and theories.

But, while we have no such teachers as those of Athens, and need no such schools as they founded, we have teachers and schools whose character and genius correspond to the age in which we live.

Teaching is a profession; not merely an ignoble pursuit, nor a toy of scholastic ambition, but a profession enjoying the public confidence, requiring great talents, demanding great industry, and securing, permit me to say, great rewards. To be the leader of a sect or the founder of a school, is something; but the acceptable teacher is superior to either; he is the first and chief exponent of a popular sovereignty which seeks happiness and immortality for itself by elevating and refining the parts of which it is composed. The ancient teacher gathered his hearers, disciples, and pupils, in the streets, groves, and public squares. The modern teacher is comparatively secluded; but let him not hence infer that he is without influence. Socrates, Plato, and Aristotle, had their triumphs; but none more distinguished than that of a Massachusetts teacher, who, at the age of fourscore years, on a festive day, received from his former pupils — and among them were the most eminent of the land — sincere and affectionate assurances of esteem and gratitude. The pupil may be estranged from the master in opinion, for our system does not concern itself with opinions, political or religious; but the faithful teacher will always find the evidence of his fidelity in the lives of those intrusted to his care. No position is more important than the teacher's; and his influence is next to that of the parent. It is his high and noble province to touch the youthful mind, test its quality, and develop its characteristics. He often stands in the place of the parent. He aids in giving character to the generations of men; which is at once a higher art and a purer glory than distinguishes those who build the walls of cities, or lay the foundations of empires. The cities which contested for the honor of being the birthplace of Homer are forgotten, or remembered only because they contested for the honor, while Homer himself is immortal. If, then, the mere birth of a human being is an honor to a city, how illustrious the distinction of those who guide the footsteps of youth along the rugged paths of learning, and develop in a generation the principles of integrity and mercy, justice and freedom, government and humanity! If in a lifetime of toil the teacher shall bring out of the mass of common minds one Franklin, or Howard, or Channing, or Bowditch, he will have accomplished more than is secured by the devotees of wealth, or the disciples of pleasure. As the man is more important than the mere philosopher, so is the modern teacher more elevated than the ancient.

The true teacher takes hold of the practical and elementary, as distinguished from the learning whose chief or sole value is in display. Present gratification is desirable, especially to parents and teachers; but it may be secured at the cost of solid learning and real progress. This is a serious error among us, and it will not readily be abandoned; but it is the duty of teachers, and of all parents who are friends to genuine learning, to aid in its removal. We are inclined to treat the period of school-life as though it covered the entire time that ought properly to be devoted to education. The first result — a result followed by pernicious consequences — is that the teacher is expected to give instruction in every branch that the pupil, as child, youth, or adult, may need to know. It is impossible that instruction so varied should always be good. Learning is knowledge of subjects based and built upon a thorough acquaintance with their elements. The path of duty, therefore, should lead the teacher to make his instruction thorough in a few branches, rather than attempt to extend it over a great variety of subjects. This, to the teacher who is employed in a district or town but three or six months, is a hard course, and many may not be inclined to pursue it. Something, no doubt, must be yielded to parents; but they, too, should be educated to a true view of their children's interests. As the world is, a well-spoken declamation is more gratifying to parents, and more creditable to teachers, than the most careful training in the vowel-sounds; yet the latter is infinitely more valuable to the scholar. Neither progress in the languages nor knowledge of mathematics can compensate for the want of a thorough etymological discipline. This training should be primary in point of time, as well as elementary in character; and a classical education is no adequate compensation.

Elements are all-important to the teacher and the student. It is not possible to have an idea of a square without some idea of a straight line, nor to express with pencil or words the arc of a circle without a previous conception of the curve. Combination follows in course. We are driven to it. Our own minds, all nature, all civilization, tend to the combination of elements.

We think fast, live fast, learn fast, and, as the fashion of the world requires a knowledge of many things, we crowd the entire education of our children into the short period of school-life. Here, and just here, public sentiment ought to relieve the teacher by reforming itself.

It should be understood that school-life is to be devoted to the thorough discipline of the mind to study, and to an acquaintance with those simple, elementary branches, which are the foundation of all good learning. When a knowledge of the elements is secured, then the languages, mathematics, and all science, may be pursued with enthusiasm and success by a class of men well educated in every department. Public sentiment must allow the teacher to give careful instruction in reading and spelling, for example, in the most comprehensive meaning of those terms — in the sound and power of letters, in the composition and use of words, and in the natural construction of sentences. This, of course, includes a knowledge of grammar, not as a dry, philological study, but as a science ; not as composed of arbitrary rules, merely, but as the common and best judgment of men concerning the use and power of language, of which rules and definitions are but an imperfect expression.

Nor do we herein assign the teacher to neglect or obscurity. He, as well as others, must have faith in the future. His reward may be distant, but it is certain.

It is, however, likely that the labors of a faithful elementary teacher will be appreciated immediately, and upon the scene of his toil. But, if they are not, his pupils, advancing in age and increasing in knowledge, will remember with gratitude and in words the self-sacrificing labors of their master.

We are not so constituted as to labor without motive. With some the motive is high, with others it is low and grovelling. The teacher must be himself elevated, or he cannot elevate others. The pupil may, indeed, advance to a higher sphere than that occupied by the teacher ; but it is only because he draws from a higher fountain elsewhere. In such cases the success of the pupil is not the success of the master. He who labors as a teacher for mere money, or for temporary fame, which is even less valuable, cannot choose a calling more ignoble, nor can he ever rise to a higher ; for his sordid motives bring all pursuits to the low level of his own nature.

Yet it is not to be assumed that the teacher, more than the clergyman, is to labor without pecuniary compensation ; for, while money should not be the sole object of any man's life, it is, under the influence of our civilization, essential to the happiness of us all. Wealth, properly acquired and properly used, may become a means of self-education. It purchases relief from the harassing toil of uninterrupted manual labor. It is the only introduction we can have to the thoroughfares of travel by which we are made acquainted personally with the globe that we inhabit. It brings to our firesides books, paintings, and statuary, by which we learn something of the world as it is and as it was. It gives us the telescope and the microscope, by whose agency we are able to appreciate, even though but imperfectly, the immensity of creation on the one hand,

and its infinity on the other. The teacher is not to labor without money, nor to despise it more than other men ; and the public might as well expect the free services of the minister, lawyer, physician, or farmer, as to expect the gratuitous or cheap education of their children. While the teacher is educating others, he must also educate himself. This he cannot do without both leisure and money. The advice of Iago is, therefore, good advice for teachers: "Go, make money. * * Put money enough in your purse." The teacher's motives should be above mere gain ; though this view of the subject does not, as some might infer, lead to the conclusion that he ought to labor for inadequate compensation.

When George III. was first insane, Dr. Willis was called to the immediate personal charge of the king. Dr. Willis had been educated to the church, and a living had been assigned him ; but, becoming interested in the subject of insanity, he had established an asylum, and gained a distinguished position in his new profession. The suffering monarch was sadly puzzled to know why Dr. Willis was with him, and how he had been brought there. The custodian was not very definite in his explanations, but suggested that he came to comfort the king in his afflictions ; and, said he, "You know that our Saviour went about doing good." — "Yes," said the king, "but he never received seven hundred pounds a year for it." This was good wit, especially good royal wit, because unexpected. But there is no reason why actual monarchs of England, or coming monarchs of America, should be treated or taught gratuitously. The compensation, the living of the teacher, is one thing; the motive may and ought to be quite different. The teacher should labor in his profession because he loves it, because he does good in it, and because he can in that sphere answer a high purpose of existence. These being the motives of the teacher, he should educate, draw out, corresponding ones in his pupils.

The teacher is not to create — he is to draw out. Every child has the germs of many, and, it may be, quite different qualities of character. Look at the infant. It is so constituted that it may have a stalwart arm, broad chest, and well-rounded, vigorous muscles; but yet it may come to adult age destitute of these physical excellences. Yet you will not say that the elements did not exist in the child. They were there; but, being neglected, they followed a law of our nature, that the development of a faculty depends upon its exercise. Nature will develop some quality in every man; for our existence demands the exercise of a part of our faculties.

The faculty used will be developed in excess as compared with other faculties. It is the business of the teacher to aid nature. For the most part, he must stimulate, encourage, draw out, develop, though it may happen that he will be required occasionally to check a tendency which threatens to absorb or overshadow all the others. He must, at any rate, prevent the growth of those powers which tend towards the savage state.

While the teacher creates nothing, he must so draw out the qualities of the child that it may attain to perfect manhood. He moulds, he renders symmetrical, the physical, the intellectual, the moral man. Nature sometimes does this herself, as though she would occasionally furnish a model man for our imitation, as she has given lines, and forms, and colors, which all artists of all ages shall copy, but cannot equal. But, do the best we can, education is more or less artificial ; and hence the child of the school will suffer by comparison with the child of nature, when she presents him in her best forms.

In a summer ramble I met a man so dignified as to attract the notice and command the respect of all who knew him. I was with him upon the lakes and mountains several days and nights, and never for a moment did the manliness of his character desert him. I have seen no other person who could boast such physical beauty. Accustomed to a hunter's life; carrying often a pack of thirty or forty or fifty pounds; sleeping upon the ground or a bed of boughs; able, if necessity or interest demanded, to travel in the woods the ordinary distance which a good horse would pass over upon our roads; with every organ of the arm, the leg, the trunk, fully expressed; with a manly, kind, intelligent countenance, a beard uncut, in the vigor of early manhood, he seemed a model which the statuaries of Greece and Rome desired to see, but did not. He had at once the bearing of a soldier and the characteristics of a gentleman. He was ignorant of grammatical rules and definitions, yet his conversation would have been accepted in good circles of New England society. This man had his faults, but they were not grievous faults, nor did they in any manner affect the qualities of which I have spoken.

This is what nature sometimes does; this is what we should always strive to do, extending this symmetry, if possible, to the moral as well as to the intellectual and physical organization. This man is ignorant of science, of books, of the world of letters, and the world of art, yet we respect him. Why? Because nature has chosen to illustrate in him her own principles, power and beauty.

That we may draw out the qualities of the human

mind as they exist, we must first appreciate our influence upon childhood and youth. Our own experience is the best evidence of what that influence is. All along our lives the lessons of childhood return to us. The hills and valleys, the lakes, rivers, and rivulets, of our early home, come not in clearer visions before us than do the exhortations to industry, the incentives to progress, the lessons of learning, and the principles of truth, uttered and offered by the teachers of early years. In the same way the lines of the poet, the reflections of the philosopher, the calm truths of the historian, read once and often carelessly, and for many years forgotten, return as voices of inspiration, and are evermore with us.

That the teacher may have influence, his ear must be open to the voice of truth, and his mouth must be liberal with words of consolation, encouragement, and advice. He rules in a little world, and the scales of justice must be balanced evenly in his hands. He should go in and out before his scholars free from partiality or prejudice; indifferent to the voice of envy or detraction; shunning evil and emulous of good; patient of inquiries in the hours of duty; filled with the spirit of industry in his moments of leisure; gathering up and spreading before his pupils the choicest gems of literature, art, and science, that they may be early and truly inspired with the love of learning.

The public school is a little world, and the teacher rules therein. It contains the rich and the poor, the virtuous and the corrupt, the studious and the indifferent, the timid and the brave, the fearful and the hearts elate with hope and courage. Life is there no cheat; it wears no mask, it assumes no unnatural positions, but presents itself as it is. Deformed and repulsive in some of its features, yet to him whose eye is as quick to discover its beauty as its deformity, its harmony as its discord, there is always a bright spot on which he may gaze, and a fond hope to which he may cling. Artificial life, whether in the select school or the select party, tends to weaken our faith in humanity; and a want of faith in our race is an omen of ill-success in life. Teachers should have faith in humanity, and should labor constantly to inspire others with the belief that the true law of our nature is the law of progress.

Those who come early in life to the conclusion that the many cannot be moved by the higher sentiments and ideas which control a few favored mortals, cease to labor for the advancement of the race. They consequently lose their hold upon society, and society neglects them. For such men there can be no success.

Others, like Jefferson and Channing, never lose confidence in their species, and their species never lose confidence in them. When the teacher comes to believe that the world is worse than it was, and never can be better, he need wait for no other evidence that his days of usefulness are over.

The school-room will teach the child, even as the prison will instruct maturity and age, that few persons are vicious in the extreme, and that no one lives without some ennobling traits of character and life. The teacher's faith is the measure of the teacher's usefulness. It is to him what conception is to the artist; and, if the sculptor can see the image of grace and beauty in the fresh-quarried marble, so must the teacher see the full form of the coming man in the trembling child or awkward youth.

The teacher ought not to grow old. To be sure, time will lay its hand on him, as it does on others; but he should always cultivate in himself the feelings, sentiments, and even ambitions of youth. Far enough removed from his pupils in age and position to stimulate them by his example, and encourage them by his precepts, he should yet be so near them that he can appreciate the steps and struggles which mark their progress in the path of learning. There must be some points of contact, something common to teacher and pupils. Indeed, for us all it is true that age loses nothing of its dignity or respect when it accepts the sentiments and sports of youth and childhood. But above all should the teacher remember the common remark of La Place, in his Celestial Mechanics, and the observation of Dr. Bowditch upon it. "Whenever I meet in La Place with the words, 'Thus it plainly appears,' I am sure that hours, and perhaps days, of hard study, will alone enable me to discover *how* it plainly appears." The good teacher will seek first to estimate each scholar's capacity, and then adapt his instructions accordingly. Though he may be far removed from his pupils in attainments, he should be able to mark the steps by which ordinary minds pass from common principles to their noblest application.

This observation may by some be deemed unnecessary; but there are living teachers who, having mastered the noblest sciences, are unable to appreciate and lead ordinary minds.

The teacher must be in earnest. This is the price of success in every profession. The law, it is said, is a jealous mistress, and permits no rivals; the indifferent, careless minister is but a blind leader of the blind, and the "undevout astronomer is mad."

Sincerity of soul and earnestness of purpose will achieve success. According to an eminent authority, there are three kinds of great men : those who are born great, those who achieve greatness, and those who have greatness thrust upon them. If we take greatness of birth to be in greatness of soul and intellect, and not in the mere accident of ancestry, it is such only who have greatness thrust upon them; for the world, after all, rarely makes a mistake in this respect. But there is a larger and a nobler class, whose greatness, whatever it is, must be achieved; and to this class I address myself.

Success is practicable. There need be no failures. A man of reflection will soon find whether he can succeed in his pursuit; if not, he has mistaken his calling, or neglected the proper means of success. In either case, a remedy is at hand. If a teacher is indifferent to his calling, and cannot bring himself to pursue it with ardor, it is a duty to himself, to his profession, to his pupils, to abandon it at once. It is idle to suppose that we are doing good in a work to which we are not attracted by our sympathies, and in which we are not sustained by our faith and hopes. The men who succeed are the men who believe that they can succeed. The men who fail are those to whom success would have been a surprise. There is no doubt some appropriate pursuit in life for every man of ordinary talents; but no one can tell whether he has found it for himself until he has made a vig-

22*

orous and persistent application of his powers. If the teacher fail to do this, he need not seek for success in another profession, when he has already declined to pay its price.

The choice of a profession is one of the great acts of life. It should not be done hastily, nor without a careful examination and just appreciation of the elements of character. A competent teacher may aid his pupils in this respect. A mistake in occupation is a calamity to the individual, and an injury to the public. Our school-rooms contain artists, farmers, mathematicians, mechanics, poets, lawyers, statesmen, orators, and warriors; but some one must do for them what Shakspeare says the monarch of the hive has done for all his subjects — assigned them

"Officers of sorts;
Where some, like magistrates, correct at home;
Others, like merchants, venture trade abroad;
Others, like soldiers, armed in their stings,
Make boot upon the summer's velvet buds;
Which pillage, they with merry march bring home
To the tent-royal of their emperor;
Who, busied in his majesty, surveys
The singing masons, building roofs of gold;
The civil citizens kneading up the honey;
The poor mechanic porters crowding in
Their heavy burdens at his narrow gate;
The sad-eyed justice, with his surly hum,

Delivering o'er to executors pale
The lazy, yawning drone."

Teachers are so situated that they may give wholesome advice; while parents — and I say it with respect — are quite likely, under the influence of an instinctive belief that their children are fitted for any place within the range of human labor or human ambition, to make fatal mistakes. While all pursuits and professions, if honest, are equally honorable, the individual selection must be determined by taste, circumstances, individual habits, and often by physical facts. It is not for one person to do everything, but it is for each person to do at least one thing well. As a general rule, the painter, who has spent his youth and manhood in studying the canvas, had better not study the stars; and the artist, who has power to bring the form of life from the cold marble, has no right to solve problems in geometry, weigh planets, or calculate eclipses. The proper choice of the business of life may do much to perfect our social system, and it will certainly advance our material prosperity. There is everywhere in our civilization mutual dependence, and there must be mutual support. In no other way can we advance to our destiny as becomes an enlightened people.

But all of life and education, either to pupil, teacher, or man, is not to be found in the school-room. The common period of school-life is sufficient only for elementary education. The average school-going period is ten years. Of this, one-half is spent in vacations and absences, so that each child has about five years of school-life. Only one-fourth of each day is spent in the school-room; and the continuous attendance, therefore, is about fifteen months, equal to the time which most of us give to sleep, every four or five years of our existence. This view leads me to say again that it is the duty of the teacher in this brief period to lay a good foundation for subsequent scientific and classical culture. More than this cannot be accomplished; and, where this is accomplished, and a taste for learning is formed, and the means to be employed are comprehended, a satisfactory school-life has been passed.

Education — universal education — is a necessity; and, as there is no royal road to learning, so there is no aristocracy of mental power depending upon social or pecuniary distinctions. The New England colonies, and Massachusetts first of all, established the system of education now called universal or public. It was not then easy to comprehend the principle which lies at the foundation of a system of public instruction. We are first to consider that a system of public instruction implies a system of universal taxation. The only rule on which taxes can be levied justly is that the object sought is of public necessity, or manifest public convenience. It quite often happens that men of our own generation are insensible or indifferent to the true relation of the citizen to the cause of education. Some seem to imagine that their interest in schools, and of course their moral obligation to support them, ceases with the education of their own children. This is a great error. The public has no right to levy a tax for the education of any particular child, or family of children ; but its right of taxation commences when the education or plan of education is universal, and ceases whenever the plan is limited, or the operations of the system are circumscribed.

No man can be taxed properly because he has children of his own to educate ; this may be a reason with some for cheerful payment, but it has in itself no element of a just principle. When, however, the people decide that education is a matter of public concern, then taxation for its promotion rests upon the same foundation as the most important departments of a government. Yet, many generations of men came and passed away before the doctrine was received that, as a public matter, a man is equally interested in the education of his neighbor's children as in the education of his own. As parents, we have a special interest in our children; as citizens, it is this, that they may be honest, industrious, and effective in their labors. This interest we have in all children.

The safety of our persons and property demands their honesty; our right to be exempt from pauper and criminal taxes requires habits of universal industry; and our part in the general wealth and prosperity is increased by the intelligent application of manual labor in all the walks of life.

A man may, indeed, be proud of the attainments of his family, as men are often proud of their ancestry; yet they possess little real value as a family possession. The pride of ancestry has no value; it

> "Is like a circle in the water,
> Which never ceaseth to enlarge itself
> Till, by broad-spreading, it disperse to naught."

I pass from this digression to the statement that the chief means of self-improvement are five: Observation, Conversation, Reading, Memory, and Reflection.

It is an art to observe well — to go through the world with our eyes open — to see what is before us. All men do not see alike, nor see the same things. Our powers of observation take on the hues of daily life. The artist, in a strange city or foreign land, observes only the specimens of taste and beauty or their opposites; the mechanic studies anew the principles of his science as applied to the purposes of life; the architect transfers to his own mind the images of churches, cathedrals, temples, and palaces; while the philanthropist rejoices in cellars and lanes, that he may know how poverty and misery change the face and heart of man.

An American artist, following the lead of Mr. Jefferson, has beautifully illustrated the nature of the power of observation. We do not see even the faces of our common friends alike. The stranger observes a family likeness which is invisible to the familiar acquaintance. The former sees only the few points of agreement, and decides upon them; while the latter has observed and studied the more numerous points of difference, until he is blind to all others. Hence a portrait may appear true to a stranger, which, to an intimate acquaintance, is barren in expression, and destitute of character. Therefore, the artist wisely and properly esteemed himself successful when his work was approved by the wife or the mother. The world around us is full of knowledge. We should so behold it as to be instructed by all that is. The distant star paints its image on our eye with a ray of light sent forth thousands of years ago; yet its lesson is not of itself, but of the universe and its mysteries, and of the Creator out of whose divine hand all things have come.

Conversation is at once an art, an accomplishment, and a science. It leads to valuable practical results. It has a place, and by no means an inferior place, in the schools. Facts stated, questions proposed, or theories illustrated, in conversation, are permanently impressed upon the mind. It is in the power of the teacher to communicate much information in this way, and it is in the power of us all to make conversation a means of improvement.

But, when the pupil leaves the school, *reading*, so systematic and thorough as to be called study, is, no doubt, the best culture he can enjoy. In the first place, books are accessible to all, and they may be had at all times. They can be used in moments of leisure, in solitude, in the hours when sleep is too proud to wait on us, and when friends are absent or indifferent to our lot. Conversation may be patronizing, or it may leave us a debtor; when the bookseller's bill is settled, we have no account with the author.

If I am permitted to speak to all, pupils as well as teachers, I am inclined to say, "Do not consider your education finished when you leave home and the school." Your labors of a practical sort ought then to commence. With system and care, you may read works of literature and history, or devote yourself to mathematics in the higher departments of science. As a general thing, however, it is not wise to attempt too much at once. The custom of the schools is to require each pupil to attend to several branches at the same time ; but this course cannot be recommended to adult persons with disciplined minds. It seems better to select one subject, and make it the leading topic, for a time, of our studies and thoughts. It may also be proper to suggest that works of fiction, poetry, and romance, ought not to be read until the mind is well disciplined, and a good foundation of solid learning is laid. Such works tend to make one's style of thought and writing easy, flowing, and agreeable ; but they are also calculated to make us dissatisfied with the more substantial labors of intellectual life. Having obtained the elements of learning, one thing is absolutely essential — system in study. I fancy that there are two prevalent errors among us. First, that men often attain intellectual eminence without study ; and, secondly, that exclusive devotion to books is the price of success. Whoever neglects study, whatever his natural abilities, will find himself distanced by inferior men ; and, on the other hand, whoever will devote three hours each day to the systematic improvement of his mind will finally be numbered among the leading persons of the age. But, while we observe, converse, and read, the power of memory and the habit of reflection should be cultivated. The habit of reflection is a great aid to the memory, and together they enable us to use the knowledge we daily acquire.

No previous age of the world has offered so great encouragement, whether in fame or money, to men of science and literature, as the present. Formerly, authors flourished under the patronage of princes, or withered by their neglect; but now they are encouraged and paid by the people, and reap where they have sown, whether kings will or not. The poverty of authors was once proverbial; but now the only authors who are poor are poor authors. Good learning, integrity, and ability, are well compensated in all the professions. Some one remarked to Mr. Webster, "That the profession of the law was crowded." —"Yes," said he, "rather crowded below, but there is plenty of room above." Littleness and mediocrity always seek the paths worn by superior men; and the truly illustrious in literature and science are few in number compared with those who attempt to tread in the footsteps of their illustrious predecessors; but none of these things ought to deter young men of ability, industry, and integrity, from boldly entering the lists, without fear of failure. The world is usually just, and it will ultimately award the tokens of its approbation to those who deserve success.

And there is a happy peculiarity in talent, — the variety is so great that the competition is small. Of all the living authors, are there two so alike that they can be considered competitors or rivals? The nation has applauded and set the seal of its approbation upon the eloquence of Henry, Otis, Adams, Ames, Pinckney, Wirt, Calhoun, Clay, and Webster, not because these men resembled one another, but because each had peculiarities and excellences of his own. The same variety of excellence is seen in living orators, and in all the eloquence and learning of antiquity which time has spared and history has transmitted to us. It is said that when Aristides wrote the sentence of his own banishment for a humble and unknown enemy, the only reason given by the peasant was that he was "tired with hearing him called the Just." And the world sometimes appears to be restive under the influence of men of talent; but that influence, whether always agreeable or not, is both permanent and beneficial.

Not only does each generation respect its own leading minds, but it is submissive to the learning and intellect of other days. The influence of ancient Greece still remains. We copy her architecture, borrow from her philosophy, admire her poetry, and bow with humility before the remnants of her majestic literature. So the policy of Rome is perceptible in the civilization of every European country, and it is a potent element in the laws and jurisprudence of America. The eloquence of Demosthenes has been impressed upon every succeeding generation of civilized men ; the genius of Hannibal has stimulated the ambition of warriors from his own time to that of Napoleon ; while Shakspeare's power has been the wonder of all modern authors and readers. It is a great representative fact in mental philosophy, which we cannot too much contemplate, that Demosthenes and Cicero not only enchained the thousands of Greece and Rome in whose presence they stood, but that their eloquence has had a controlling influence over myriads to whom the language in which they spoke was unknown. The words that the houseless Homer sung in the streets of Smyrna have commanded the admiration of all later times ; and even the mud walls around Plato's garden, on which are preserved the fragments of statuary with which the garden was once adorned, attract and instruct the wanderers and students about Athens.

But let us not deceive ourselves with the idea that we can illustrate anew the greatness which has distinguished a few men only in all the long centuries of the world's existence. Be not imitators nor followers of other men's glory. There is a path for each one, and his duty lies therein. Yet the leading men of the world are lights which ought not to be hid from the young, for they serve to show the extent of the field in which human powers may be employed. The rule of the successful life is to neglect no present opportunity of good either to yourself or to others; and the rule of the successful student is to gather information from whatever source he may, not doubting that it will prove useful to himself or to his fellow-men.

Our own age has furnished two men, — one living, the other dead, — quite opposite in talents and attainments, whose power and influence may not have been surpassed in ancient or modern times. I speak of Kossuth and Webster. Our history has no parallel for the first. Most men, young or old, gay or severe, radical or conservative, were touched by his mournful strains, and influenced by his magic words. He came from a land of which we knew little, and so laid open the history of its wrongs that he enlisted multitudes in its behalf. I speak not now of the views he presented, nor of the demands he made upon the American people. If he taught error and asked wrong, so the more wonderful was his career. No doubt his cause did much for him;

but other patriots and exiles have had equal opportunities with Kossuth, yet no one has so swayed the public mind.

He was distinguished in intellect, a master of much learning, a man of nice moral feeling and strong religious sentiments, all of which were combined and blended in his addresses to the people. But he spoke a language whose rudiments he first learned in manhood. In his speech he neglected the chief rule of Grecian eloquence. With one theme, only, — the wrongs of Hungary; with one object, only, — her relief and elevation, — he commanded the general attention of the American mind. The mission of Kossuth in America deserves to be remembered as an intellectual phenomenon, whose like, we of this generation may not again see.

Mr. Webster had never great personal popularity. His presence was majestic, but forbidding. His manners were agreeable, and sometimes fascinating to his friends, when he was in a genial mood; but he was often reserved or even austere to strangers, and terrible to his enemies. His style of thought was mathematical, his language expressive, but never popular. He wrote as a man would dictate an essay which was to appear as a posthumous work. His eloquence was not that which often passes for eloquence upon the stump or at the bar. He seldom attempted to court the people, and when he did, it was as if he mocked himself, and scorned the spirit which could be moved by the breezes of popular favor. He was not free from faults, personal and political; yet he acquired a control which has not been possessed by any man since Washington. Whenever he was to speak, the public were anxious to hear and to read. Hardly any man has had the fortune to present his views in addresses, letters, and speeches, to so large a portion of his countrymen; yet the people whom he addressed, and who were anxious for his words and opinions, did not always, or even generally, agree with him. Mr. Webster's power was chiefly, if not solely, intellectual. He had not the personal qualities of Mr. Clay or General Jackson; he was not, like Mr. Jefferson, the chosen exponent of a political creed, and the admitted leader of a great political party; nor had he the military character and universally acknowledged patriotism of General Washington, which made him first in the hearts of his countrymen. Mr. Webster stands alone. His domain is the intellect, and thus far in America he is without a rival. To Mr. Webster, and to all men proportionately, according to the measure of their gifts and attainments, we may apply his great words: "A superior and commanding human intellect, a truly great man, when Heaven vouchsafes so rare a gift, is not a temporary flame, burning brightly for a while, and then giving place to returning darkness. It is rather a spark of fervent heat, as well as radiant light, with power to enkindle the common mass of human mind; so that, when it glimmers in its own decay, and finally goes out in death, no night follows, but it leaves the world all light, all on fire, from the potent contact of its own spirit."

Some humble measure of this greatness may be attained by all; and, if I have sought to lead you in the way of improvement by considerations too purely personal and selfish, I will implore you, in conclusion, as teachers and as citizens, to consider yourselves as the servants of your country and your race. There can be no real greatness of mind without generosity of soul. If a superior human intellect seems to be specially the gift of God, how is he wanting in true religion who fails to dedicate it to humanity, justice, and virtue!

An eminent historian, seeing at one view, and as in the present moment, the fall of great states, ancient and modern, and anticipating a like fate for his own beloved land, has predicted that in two centuries there will be three hundred millions of people in North America speaking the language of England, reading its authors, and glorying in their descent.

If this be so, what limits can we assign to the work, or how estimate the duty, of those intrusted with the education of the young?

Who can say what share of responsibility for the future of America is upon the teachers of the land?

LIBERTY AND LEARNING.

[An Address delivered at Montague, July 4th, 1857.]

I CONGRATULATE you upon the auspicious moments of this, the eighty-first anniversary of our National Independence ; and its return, now and ever, should be the occasion of gratitude to the Author of all good, that He hath vouchsafed to our fathers and to their descendants the wisdom to establish and the wisdom to preserve the institutions of Liberty in America.

And I congratulate you that you accept this anniversary as the occasion for considering the subject of education. Ignorant and blind worshippers of Liberty can do but little for its support ; but, whatever of change or decay may come to our institutions, Liberty itself can never die in the presence of a people universally and thoroughly educated. It is not, then, inappropriate nor unphilosophical for us to connect Education and Liberty together ; and I therefore propose, after presenting some thoughts upon the Declaration of Independence, and its relations to the American Union, to consider the value of political learning, its neglect, and the means by which it may be promoted.

The events and epochs of life are logical in their nature, and are harmonious or inharmonious as the affairs of men are controlled by principle, policy, or accident. Humboldt, Maury, and Guyot, Arago, Agassiz, and Pierce, by observation, philosophy, and mathematics, demonstrate the harmony of the physical creation. In the microscopic animalculæ; in the gigantic remains, whether vegetable or animal, of other ages and conditions of life; in the coral reef and the mountain range; in the hill-side rivulet that makes "the meadows green;" in the ocean current that bathes and vivifies a continent; in the setting of the leaf upon its stem, and the moving of Uranus in its orbit, they trace a law whose harmony is its glory, and whose mystery is the evidence of its divinity.

National changes, the movements and progress of the human race, as a whole and in its parts, are obedient, likewise, to law; and are, therefore, logical in their character, though generally lacking in precision of connection and order of succession. Or it may be, rather, that we lack power to trace the connection between events that depend in part, at least, upon the prejudices, passions, vices, and weaknesses, of men. The development of the logic of human affairs waits for a philosopher who shall study and comprehend the living millions of our race, as the philosophers now study and comprehend the subjects of physical science. We have no guaranty that this can ever be done. As mind is above matter, the mental philosopher enters upon the most varied and difficult field of labor.

Keeping this fact in mind, it appears to be true that every person of observation, reading, and reflection, is something of a mental philosopher, though much the larger number have no knowledge of physical science. And especially must the student of history have a system of mental philosophy; but often, no doubt, his system is too crude for general notice. Every historian connects the events of his narrative by some thread of philosophy or speculation; every reader observes some connection, though he may never develop it to himself, between the events and changes of national and ethnological life; and even the observer whose vision is limited by his own horizon in time and space marks a dependence, and speaks of cause and effect. All this follows from the existence and nature of man. Man is not inert, nor even passive, merely; and his activity will continually organize itself into facts and forms, ever changing in character, it may be, yet subject to a law as wise and fixed as that of planetary motion.

The Independence of the British Colonies in America, declared on the 4th of July, 1776, is not an isolated fact; nor is the Declaration itself a hasty and overwrought production of a young and enthusiastic adventurer in the cause of liberty.

The passions and the reason of men connected the Declaration of Independence with the massacre in King-street, of March 5th, 1770; with the passage and repeal of the Stamp Act; with the attempt to enforce the Writs of Assistance; with the act to close the port of Boston; with the peace of 1763; with the Act of Settlement of 1688; with the execution of Charles I., and the Protectorate of Cromwell; with the death of Hampden; with the confederation of 1643; with the royal charters granted to the respective colonies; with the compact made on board the Mayflower; and, finally, and distinctly, and chiefly, — as the basis of the greatest legal argument of modern times, made by the Massachusetts House of Representatives, from 1765 to 1775, — with the events at Runnymede, and the grant of the Great Charter to the nobles and people of England in 1215, which is itself based upon the concessions of Edward the Confessor, and the affirmation of the Saxon laws in the eleventh century. Our Independence is, then, one logical fact or event in a long succession, to the enumeration of which we may yet add the confederation of 1778, the constitution of 1787, the French Revolution of 1789, the rapid increase of American territory and States, the revolutionary spirit of continental Europe, the reforms in the British government at home, the wise modifications of its colonial policy, and for us a long career of prosperity based upon the cardinal doctrine of the equality of all men before the law.

Nor can any reader of the Declaration itself assume that it contains one statement, proposition, idea, or word, not carefully considered, and carefully expressed. It was not the production of hasty, thoughtless, or reckless men. The country had been gradually prepared for the great event. States, counties, and towns, had made the most distinct expressions of opinion upon the relations of the colonies to the mother country. On the 7th of June, 1776, Richard Henry Lee, of Virginia, moved, in the Congress of the United Colonies, a resolution declaring, That these United Colonies are, and of right ought to be, free and independent states ; that they are absolved from all allegiance to the British crown, and that all political connection between them and the state of Great Britain is, and ought to be, totally dissolved. The subject was considered on the tenth ;

and, on the eleventh instant, the committee, consisting of Thomas Jefferson, John Adams, Dr. Franklin, Roger Sherman, and Robert R. Livingston, was appointed. On the twenty-fifth of June, a Declaration of the Deputies of Pennsylvania, in favor of Independence, was read. On the twenty-eighth, the credentials of the delegates from New Jersey, in which they were instructed to favor Independence, were presented ; and on the first of July similar instructions to the Maryland delegates were laid before Congress. At this time Congress proceeded to consider the Declaration and resolution reported by the committee. The Declaration was carefully considered, and materially amended in committee of the whole, on the first, second, third, and fourth, when it was finally adopted. It was then signed by the president and secretary, and copies were transmitted to the several colonies. The order for its engrossment, and for the signature by every member, was not passed until the nineteenth of July, and it was not really signed until the second of August following. It is not likely, considering the circumstances, and the known character of the members of Congress, among whom may be mentioned John Hancock, Samuel Adams, Benjamin Rush, Robert Morris, Benjamin Harrison, Elbridge Gerry, John Witherspoon, a descendant of John Knox, the Scottish Reformer, Charles Carroll, and Samuel Huntington, — all distinguished for coolness, probity, and patriotism, — that the immortal document can contain one thought or word unworthy its sacred associations, and the character of the American people!

And it is among the alarming symptoms of public sentiment that the Declaration of Independence is by some publicly condemned, and by others quietly accepted as entitled to just the consideration, and no more, that is given to an excited advocate's speech to a jury, or a demagogue's electioneering harangue, or the daily contribution of the partisan editor to the stock of political capital that aids the election of his favorite candidates. And upon this evidence is the nation and the world to be taught that but little was meant by the assertions, "that all men are created equal; that they are endowed by their Creator with certain inalienable rights; that among these are life, liberty, and the pursuit of happiness; that, to secure these rights, governments are instituted among men, deriving their just powers from the consent of the governed"? Would it not be wiser to test the government we have, by a statesmanlike application of the principles of the Declaration of Independence in the management of public affairs?

The Union is connected with the Declaration of

Independence. The Union is an institution: the Declaration of Independence is an assertion of rights, and an exposition of principles. When principles are disregarded, institutions do not, for any considerable time, retain their original value. And it would be the folly of other nations, without excuse in us, were we to worship blindly any institution, whatever its origin or its history. I do not, myself, doubt the value of the American Union. It was the necessity of the time when it was formed; it is the necessity of the present moment; it was, indeed, the claim of our whole colonial life, and its recognition could be postponed no longer when the colonies crossed the threshold of national existence.

The colonies had carried on a correspondence among themselves upon important matters; the New England settlements formed a confederation in 1643, that was the prototype of the present Union; and the convention at Albany, in 1754, considered in connection with various resolutions and declarations, indicated a growing desire "to form a more perfect union, establish justice, insure domestic tranquillity, provide for the common defence, promote the general welfare, and secure the blessings of liberty" to the successive generations that should occupy the American continent.

For these exalted purposes the Constitution was

framed, and the Union established; and the Constitution and the Union will remain as long as these exalted purposes, with any considerable share of fidelity, are secured. The Union will not be destroyed by declamation, nor can declamation preserve it. Words have power only when they awaken a response in the minds of those who listen. The Union will be judged, finally, by its merits; and they are not powerful enemies for evil who attack it through the press and from the rostrum; but rather they who, clothed with authority, brief or permanent, interpret the constitution so as to defeat the end for which it was framed. Nor are they the best friends of the Union who lavishly bestow upon it nicely-wrought encomiums, as though the gilding of rhetoric and the ornament of praise could shield a human institution from the judgment of a free people; but rather they who, under Heaven, and in the presence of men, seek to so interpret the constitution as, in the language and in the order of its preamble, "to form a more perfect union, establish justice, insure domestic tranquillity, provide for the common defence, promote the general welfare, and secure the blessings of liberty" to themselves and their posterity. Words are powerless, and enemies — envious, jealous, or deluded — are powerless, when they war upon a system of government that secures such exalted results. And, if in these later days of our national existence patriotism has been weakened, respect and reverence for the constitution and the Union have been diminished, it is because the actual government under the constitution has, in the judgment of many, failed to realize the government of the constitution.

But let no one despair of the Republic. Men are now building better than they know; possibly, better than they wish. A great government, powerful in its justice, and therefore to be respected and maintained, must also be powerful in its errors, prejudices, and wrongs, and therefore to be changed and reformed in these respects. The declaration "that all men are created equal" is vital, and will live in the presence of all governments, strong as well as weak, hostile as well as friendly. It has no respect for worldly authority, so evidently is it a direct emanation of the Divine Mind, and so does it harmonize with the highest manifestations of the nature of man. But the Declaration of Independence does not, in this particular, assert that all men are created equal in height or weight, equal in physical strength, intellectual power, or moral worth. It is not dealing with these qualities at all, but with the natural political rights and relations of men. In its view, all are born free from any political subordination to others on account of the accidents or incidents of family or historic name. And hence it follows that no man, by birth or nature, has any right in political affairs to control his fellow-man; and hence it follows further, as there is neither subjection anywhere nor authority anywhere, that all men are created equal, that governments derive their "just powers from the consent of the governed." And hence it must, ere long, be demonstrated by this country, under the light of Christianity, and in the presence of the world, that man cannot have property in his fellow-man.

And, again, let no one despair of the Republic or of the Union; nor let any, with rash confidence, believe that they are indestructible. They are human institutions built up through great sacrifices, and by the exercise of a high order of worldly wisdom. But the government is not an end — it is a means. The end is Liberty regulated by law; and the means will exist as long as the end thereof is attained. But, should the time ever come when the institutions of the country fail to secure the blessings of liberty to the living generation, and hold out no promise of better things in the future, I know not that these institutions could longer exist, or that they ought longer to exist. To be sure, the horizon is not always distinctly seen. The sky is not always clear ; there are dark spots upon the disk of Liberty, as upon the sun in the heavens ; but, like the sun, its presence is for all. And, whether there be night, or clouds, or distance, its blessings can never be wholly withdrawn from the human race.

It is not to be concealed, however, that the affections of the people have been alienated from the American Union during the last seven years, as they were from the union with Great Britain during the years of our colonial life immediately previous to the Massacre in King-street, in 1770. This solemn personal and public experience is fraught with a great lesson. It should teach those who are intrusted with the administration of public affairs to translate the language of the constitution into the stern realities of public policy, in the light of the Declaration of Independence, and of Liberty ; and it should warn those who constitute the government, and who judge it, not to allow their opposition to men or to measures to degenerate into indifference or hostility to the institutions of the country.

A little distrust of ourselves, who see not beyond our own horizon, might sometimes lend charity to our judgment, and discretion to our opposition ; for, in the turmoil of politics, and the contests of statesmanship, even, it is not always

"—— the sea that sinks and shelves,
But ourselves,
That rock and rise
With endless and uneasy motion,
Now touching the very skies,
Now sinking into the depths of ocean."

And, as there must be in every society of men something of evil that can be traced to the government, and something of good neglected that a wise and efficient government might have accomplished, it is easy to build up an argument against an existing government, however good when compared with others. This is a narrow, superficial, unsatisfactory, dangerous view to take of public affairs.

We should seek to comprehend the relations of the government, the principles on which it is founded; and, while we justly complain of its defects, and seek to remedy them, we ought also to compare it with other systems that exist, or that might be established. This proposition involves an intelligent realization by the people of the character of their institutions; and I am thus led to express the apprehension that the popular political education of our day is inferior to that of the revolutionary era, and of the age that immediately succeeded it.

There is, no doubt, a disposition and a tendency to extol the recent past. The recollections of childhood are quite at variance with the real truth, and tradition is often the dream of old age concerning the events of early life. As rivers, hills, mountains, roads, and towns, are all magnified by the visions of childhood, it is not strange that men should be also. Hence comes, in part, the popular belief in the superior physical strength and greater longevity of the people who lived fifty or a hundred years ago. Each generation is familiar with its predecessor; but of the one next remote it knows only the marked characters. Those who possessed great physical excellences remain; but they are not so much the representatives of their generation as its exceptions. The weak, the diseased, have fallen by the way; and, as there is an intimate connection between physical and intellectual power, the remnant of any generation, whatever its common character, will retain a disproportionate number of strong-minded men. Hence it is not safe to judge a generation as a whole by those who remain at the age of sixty or seventy years; especially if we reflect that public opinion and tradition are most likely to preserve the names and qualities of those who were distinguished for physical or mental power. Yet, after making due allowance for these exaggerations, I cannot escape the conclusion that we have, as a people, deteriorated in average sound political learning; and I proceed to mention some of the causes and evidences of our degeneracy, and of the superiority of our ancestors.

I. *The political condition of the country has been essentially changed.* — General personal and family comfort, according to the ideas now entertained, was not a feature of American society for one hundred and seventy years from the settlement at Plymouth. Life was a continual contest — a contest with the forest, with the climate, with the Indians, and especially was it a continual contest with the mother country. The colonists sought to maintain their own rights without infringement, while they accorded to the sovereign his constitutional privileges. Conflicts were frequent, and apprehensions of conflict yet more frequent. Hence those who had the conduct of public affairs were compelled to give some attention to English history, and to the constitutional law of Great Britain. Moreover, it was always important to secure and keep a strong public sentiment on the side of liberty; and there were usually in every town men who thoroughly investigated questions of public policy. There was one topic, more absorbing than any other, that involved the study of the legal history and usage of Great Britain, and a careful consideration of the general principles of liberty; namely, the constitutional rights of a British subject. Here was a broad field for inquiry, investigation, and study; and it was faithfully cultivated and gleaned. There has never been a political topic for public discussion in America more important in itself, or better calculated to educate an American in a knowledge of his political rights, than the examination of the political relations of the subject to the crown and parliament of Great Britain previous to the Declaration of Independence. It was not an abstraction. It had a practical value to every man in the colonies, and it was the prominent feature of the masterly exposition made by the Massachusetts House of Representatives, to which I have already referred. And we can better estimate the political education which the times furnished, when we consider that the revolutionary war was made logical and necessary through a knowledge of positions, facts, and arguments, scattered over the history of the colonies. But, when our Independence had been established and recognized, constitutions had been framed, and the governments of the states and nation set in motion, the beauty and harmony of our political system seemed to render continued attention to political principles and the rights of individual men unnecessary. Hence, we may anticipate the judgment of impartial history in the admission that public attention was gradually given to contests for office which did not always involve the maintenance of a fundamental principle of government, or the recognition of an essential human right. It does not, however, follow, from this admission, that we are indifferent to our political lot, — occasional contests upon principle refute such a conjecture, — but that men are not anxious concerning those things which appear to be secure. And the differences of political parties of the last fifty years have not been so much concerning the nature of human rights, as in regard to the institutions by which those rights can be best protected. Therefore our political questions have been questions of expediency rather than of principle. And, if there is any foundation for the popular impression that public offices are conferred on men less eminently qualified to give dignity to public employments, the reason of this degeneracy — less noteworthy than it is usually represented — is to be found in this connection.

Governments and political organizations accept the common law of society. When an individual or a corporation is prosperous, places of trust and emolument are often gained and occupied by unworthy men ; but, when profits are diminished, or when they disappear entirely; when dividends are passed, when loss and bankruptcy are imminent, then, if hope and courage still remain, places of importance are filled by the appointment of abler and worthier men.

The charge made against official character, to whatever extent true, is better evidence of confidence and prosperity than it is of the degeneracy of the people; and a public exigency, serious and long-continued, would call to posts of responsibility the highest talent and integrity which the country could produce. But it is, nevertheless, to be admitted as a necessary consequence of the facts already stated, and the views presented, that the average amount of sound political learning among those engaged in public employments is less than it was during the revolutionary era. It is, however, also to be observed, that, when such learning seems to be specially required, the people demand it and secure it. Hence the work of framing constitutions, even in the new states, has, in its execution, commanded the approval of political writers in this country and in Europe. And it must, also, be admitted that peace and prosperity render sound political learning and great experience less necessary, and at the same time multiply the number of men who are considered eligible to office. Candidates are put in nomination and elected because they have been good neighbors, honorable citizens, competent teachers of youth, or faithful spiritual guides; or, possibly, because they have been successful in business, are of the military or of the fire department, or because they are leaders and benefactors of special classes of society. In ordinary times these facts are all worthy of consideration and real deference ; but when, as in the Revolution, every place of public service is a post of responsibility, or sacrifice, or danger, candidates and electors will not meet upon these grounds, but, disregarding such circumstances, the canvass will have special reference to the work to be done. For civil employments, political learning and experience are required ; and for military posts, skill, sagacity, and courage. It may be said that our whole colonial life was a preparatory school for the revolutionary contest ; and, therefore, the major part of the enterprise, ambition, and patriotism, of the country, was given to the training, studies, and pursuits, calculated to fit men for so stern a struggle. But now that other avenues are inviting in themselves, and promise political preferment, we are liable to the criticism that our young men, well educated in the schools and in a knowledge of the world, are not well grounded in political history and constitutional law, without which there can be no thorough and comprehensive statesmanship. And, as I pass from this branch of my subject, I may properly say that I do not seek to limit the number of candidates for public office ; for every office is a school, and the public itself is a great and wise teacher. Nor do I ask any to abandon the employments and duties, or to neglect the claims of business and of social life; but I seek to impress upon our youth a sense of the importance of adding something thereto. The knowledge of which I have spoken is valuable in the ordinary course of public business, and absolutely essential in the exigences of political and national life. And it is with an eye single to the happiness of individuals, and the welfare of the public, that I invite my fellow-citizens, and especially the young men of the state, to take something from the hours of labor, where labor is excessive; or something from amusement, where amusement has ceased to be recreation; or something from light reading, which often is neither true, nor reasonable, nor useful; or something from indolence and dissipation; and, in the minutes and hours thus gained, treasure up valuable knowledge for the circumstances and exigences of citizenship and public office.

II. *The claims of business and society are unfavorable to political learning.* — I assume it to be true of Massachusetts that the proportion of freehold farmers to the whole population is gradually diminishing, and that the amount of labor performed by each is gradually increasing. From the settlement of the country to the commencement of the present century, there was a great deal of privation, hardship, and positive suffering; but the claim for continuous labor was not exacting.

The necessary articles of food and clothing were chiefly supplied from the land, and the majority did not contemplate any great accumulation of worldly goods, but sought rather to place their political and religious privileges upon a sure foundation. Agriculture was in a rude state, and consequently did not furnish steady employment to those engaged in it. It is only when there are valuable markets, scientific, or at least careful cultivation, and large profits, that the farmer can use his evenings and long winters in his profession. These circumstances did not exist until the present century; and we have thus in this discussion found both the motive and the opportunity for political learning among our ancestors.

It is also possible that the increased activity of business and business men is unfavorable to those studies and thoughts that are essential to political learning. Commerce and trade are stimulated by never-ceasing competition; and manufacturers are not free from the influence of markets, and the necessity of variety, taste, and skill, in the management of their business. If the larger share of the physical and mental vigor of a man is given to business, his hours of leisure must be hours of relaxation; and to most minds the study of history and of kindred topics is by no means equivalent to recreation. Moreover, society presents numerous claims which are not easily disregarded. Fashionable life puts questions that but few people have the courage to answer in the negative. Have you read the last novel? the new play? the reviews of the quarter? the magazines of the month? or the greatest satire of the age? These questions have puzzled many young men into customary neglect of useful reading, that they may not admit their ignorance in the presence of those whom they respect or admire.

But, everything valuable is expensive, and learning can be secured only by severe self-sacrifice. With our ancestors, after religious culture, historical and political reading was next immediately before them; but the youth of this generation who seek such learning are compelled to make their way without deference to the daily customs of society. There is no fashionable or tolerated society that invites young men to read the history of England prior to the time when Macaulay begins. Nor does public sentiment recommend De Lolme on the British constitution, the Federalist, the writings of Jefferson, Madison, Marshall, Story, and Webster, upon the constitution of the United States, and the practice of the government under it. Not but that these topics are considered in the higher institutions of learning; but I address myself to those who have enjoyed the advantages of our common schools only, where thorough instruction in national and general political history cannot be given. This kind of learning must be self-acquired, and acquired by some temporary sacrifice; and the sooner, in the case of every young man, this sacrifice is contemplated and offered, the more acceptable and useful it will be. And the acquisition of this kind of learning does not, in a majority of cases, admit of delay. It should be the work of youth and early manhood. The duties of life are so constant and pressing that we find it difficult to abstract ourselves and our thoughts from the world; but, from the age of sixteen to the age of twenty-five, the attention may be concentrated upon special subjects, and their elements mastered.

By the Athenian law, minority terminated at the age of sixteen years; and Demosthenes, at that period of his life, commenced a course of self-education by which he became the first orator of Athens, and the admiration of the after-world. The father of Demosthenes died worth fourteen talents; and the son, though defrauded by his guardians, was, as his father had been, enrolled in the wealthiest class of citizens; yet he did not hesitate to subject himself to the severest mental and physical discipline, in preparation for the great life he was to lead.

"Demosthenes received, during his youth, the ordinary grammatical and rhetorical education of a wealthy Athenian. . . . . It appears also that he was, from childhood, of sickly constitution and feeble muscular frame ; so that, partly from his own disinclination, partly from the solicitude of his mother, he took little part, as boy or youth, in the exercises of the palæstra. . . . . Such comparative bodily disability probably contributed to incite his thirst for mental and rhetorical acquisitions, as the only road to celebrity open. But it at the same time disqualified him from appropriating to himself the full range of a comprehensive Grecian education, as conceived by Plato, Isokrates, and Aristotle ; an education applying alike to thought, word, and action — combining bodily strength, endurance, and fearlessness, with an enlarged mental capacity, and a power of making it felt by speech.

"The disproportion between the physical energy and the mental force of Demosthenes, beginning in childhood, is recorded and lamented in the inscription placed on his statue after his death. . . . . Demosthenes put himself under the teaching of Isæus ; . . . . and also profited largely by the discourse of Plato, of Isokrates, and others. As an ardent aspirant, he would seek instruction from most of the best sources, theoretical as well as practical — writers as well as lecturers. But, besides living teachers, there was one of the last generation who contributed largely to his improvement. He studied Thucydides with indefatigable labor and attention; according to one account, he copied the whole history eight times over with his own hand; according to another, he learnt it all by heart, so as to be able to rewrite it from memory, when the manuscript was accidentally destroyed. Without minutely criticizing these details, we ascertain, at least, that Thucydides was the peculiar object of his study and imitation. How much the composition of Demosthenes was fashioned by the reading of Thucydides, reproducing the daring, majestic, and impressive phraseology, yet without the overstrained brevity and involutions of that great historian, — and contriving to blend with it a perspicuity and grace not inferior to Lysias,—may be seen illustrated in the elaborate criticism of the rhetor Dionysius.

"While thus striking out for himself a bold and original style, Demosthenes had still greater difficulties to overcome in regard to the external requisites of an orator. He was not endowed by nature, like Æschines, with a magnificent voice; nor, like Demades, with a ready flow of vehement improvisation.

His thoughts required to be put together by careful preparation; his voice was bad, and even lisping; his breath short; his gesticulation ungraceful; moreover, he was overawed and embarrassed by the manifestations of the multitude. . . . . The energy and success with which Demosthenes overcame his defects, in such manner as to satisfy a critical assembly like the Athenians, is one of the most memorable circumstances in the general history of self-education. Repeated humiliation and repulse only spurred him on to fresh solitary efforts for improvement. He corrected his defective elocution by speaking with pebbles in his mouth; he prepared himself to overcome the noise of the assembly by declaiming in stormy weather on the sea-shore of Phalerum; he opened his lungs by running, and extended his powers of holding breath by pronouncing sentences in marching up-hill; he sometimes passed two or three months without interruption in a subterranean chamber, practising night and day either in composition or declamation, and shaving one-half of his head in order to disqualify himself from going abroad." * Yet all this effort and sacrifice were accompanied by repeated and humiliating failures; and it was not until he was twenty-seven years of age that the great orator of the world

* Grote's Hist., vol. xi., p. 266, et seq.

achieved his first success before the Athenian assembly.

But how can the youth of this age hope to be followers, even at a distance, of Demosthenes, and of those his peers, who, by eloquence, poetry, art, science, and general learning, have added dignity to the race, and given lustre to generations separated by oceans and centuries, unless they are animated by a spirit of progress, and cheered by a faith that shall be manifested in the disposition and the power to overcome the obstacles that lie in every one's path?

Such a course of training requires individual effort and personal self-sacrifice. It would not be wise to follow the plan of the Athenian orator; he adapted his training to his personal circumstances, and the customs of the country. His history is chiefly valuable for the lessons of self-reliance, and the example of perseverance under discouragements, that it furnishes. But it is always a solemn duty to hold up before youth noble models of industry, perseverance, and success, that they may be stimulated to the work of life by the assurance of history that,

> "Not enjoyment, and not sorrow,
> Is our destined end or way;
> But to act, that each to-morrow
> Find us further than to-day."

III. *The popular reading of the day does not contribute essentially to the education of the citizen and statesman.* — It is not, of course, expected that every man is to qualify himself for the life of a statesman; but it does seem necessary for all to be so well instructed in political learning as to possess the means of forming a reasonable and philosophical opinion of the policy of the government. It is as discreditable to the intellect and judgment of a free people to complain of that which is right in itself, and rests upon established principles of right, as to submit without resistance or murmur to usurpation or misgovernment. I do not mean to undervalue the periodical press; but it must always assume something in regard to its readers, and in politics it must assume that the principles of government and the history of national institutions are known and understood.

But the young man should subject himself to a systematic course of training; and I know of nothing more valuable in political studies than a thorough acquaintance with English history. Our principles of government were derived from England; and it is in the history of the mother country that the best discussion of principles is found, as in that country many of the contests for liberty occurred. But, as our government is the outgrowth rather than a copy of British principles and institutions, the American citizen is not prepared for his duties until he has made himself familiar with American history, in all its departments. How ill-suited, then, for the duties of citizenship and public life, in the formation of taste and habits of thought, is much of the reading of the present time! And I may here call attention to the fact that each town in Massachusetts is invested with authority to establish a public library by taxation. This, it seems to me, is one of the most important legislative acts of the present decennial period; and, indeed, a public library is essential to the view I am taking of the necessity and importance of political education. Private libraries exist, but they are not found in every house, nor can every person enjoy their advantages. Public libraries are open to all; and, when the selection of books is judicious, they furnish opportunities for education hardly less to be prized than the common schools themselves. The public library is not only an aid to general learning, a contributor to political intelligence and power, but it is an efficient supporter of sound morals, and all good neighborhood among men.

If the public will not offer to its youth valuable reading, such as its experience, its wisdom, its knowledge of the claims of society, its morality may select, shall the public complain if its young men and women are tempted by frivolous and pernicious mental occupations? It is, moreover, the duty of the public to furnish the means of self-education, especially in the science of government; and political learning, for the most part, must be gained after the school-going period of life has passed.

Let American liberty be an intelligent liberty, and therefore a self-sustaining liberty. Freedom, more or less complete, has been found in two conditions of life. Man, in a rude state, where his condition seemed to be normal, rather than the result of a process of mental and moral degeneracy, has often possessed a large share of independence; but this should by no means be confounded with what in America is called liberty. The independence of the savage, or nomad, is manifested in the absence of law; but the liberty of an American citizen is the power to do whatever may be beneficial to himself, and not injurious to his neighbor nor to the state. The first leaves self-protection and self-regulation to the individual, while the latter restrains the aggressive tendencies of all for the security of each. The first is natural equality without law; the second is natural equality before the law. With the first, might makes right; with the latter, right makes might. With the first, the power of the law, or of the will of an individual or clan, is in the rigor and success of execution ; with the latter, the power of the law is in the justice of its demand. We, as a people, have passed the savage and nomadic state, and can return to it only after a long and melancholy process of decay and change, out of which ultimately might come a new and savage race of men. This, then, is not our immediate, even if it be a possible danger. But we are to guard against intellectual, political, and moral degeneracy. We are, through family, religious, and public education, to take security of the childhood and youth of the land for the preservation of the institutions we have, and for the growth, greatness, and justice, of the republic. Liberty in America, if you will admit the distinction, is a growth and not a creation. The institutions of liberty in America have the same character. By many centuries of trial, struggle, and contest, through many years of experience, sometimes joyous, and sometimes sad, the fact and the institutions of liberty in America have been evolved. It has not been a work of destruction and creation, but a process of change and progress. And so it must ever be. Reformation does not often follow destruction ; and they who seek to destroy the institutions of a country are not its friends in fact, however they may be in purpose. Ignorance can destroy, but intelligence is required to reform or build up. Let the prejudice against learning, not common now, but possibly existing in some minds, be forever banished. Learning is the friend of liberty. Of this America has had evidence in her own history, and in her observation of the experience of others. The literary institutions and the cultivated men of America, like Milton and Hampden in England, preferred

> " Hard liberty before the easy yoke
> Of servile pomp."

It was the intelligence of the country that everywhere uttered and everywhere accepted the declaration of the town of Boston, in the revolutionary struggle, " We can endure poverty, but we disdain slavery." Ignorance is quicksand on which no stable political structure can be built; and I predict the future greatness of our beloved state, in those historical qualities that outlast the ages, from the fact that she is not tempted by her extent of territory, salubrity of climate, fertility of soil, or by the presence and promise of any natural source of wealth, to falter in her devotion to learning and liberty. And I anticipate for Massachusetts a career of influence beneficial to all, whether disputed or accepted, when I reflect that, with less good fortune in the presence and combination of learning and liberty, Greece, Rome, Venice, Holland, and England, enjoyed power disproportionate to their respective populations, territory, and natural resources. And, while the object for which we are convened may pardon something to local attachments and state pride, the day and the occasion ought not to pass without a grateful and hearty acknowledgment of the interest manifested by other states and sections in the cause of general learning, and especially in common-school education. The Canadas are our rivals; the states of the West are our rivals; the states of the South are our rivals; and, were our greater experience and better opportunities reckoned against us, I know not that there would be much in our systems of education of which we could properly boast. It is, indeed, possible that North Carolina, untoward circumstances having their due weight, has made more progress in education, since 1840, than any other state of the Union.

Education is not only favorable to liberty, but, when associated with liberty, it is the basis of the Union and power of the American states. As citizens of the republic, we need a better knowledge of our national institutions, a better knowledge of the institutions of the several states, a more intimate acquaintance with one another, and the power of judging wisely and justly the policies and measures of each and all. These ends, aided or accomplished by general learning, will so strengthen the Union as no force of armies can—will so strengthen the Union as that by no force of armies can it be overthrown.

MASSACHUSETTS SCHOOL FUND.

[Extract from the Twenty-Second Annual Report of the Secretary of the Board of Education.]

The Massachusetts School Fund was established by the Legislature of 1834 (stat. 1834, chap. 169), and it was provided by the act that all moneys in the treasury on the first of January, 1835, derived from the sale of lands in the State of Maine, and from the claim of the state on the government of the United States for military services, and not otherwise appropriated, together with fifty per centum of all moneys thereafter to be received from the sale of lands in Maine, should be appropriated to constitute a permanent fund, for the aid and encouragement of Common Schools. It was provided that the fund should never exceed one million of dollars, and that the income only should be appropriated to the object in view. The mode of distribution was referred to a subsequent Legislature. It was, however, provided that a greater sum should never be paid to any city or town than was raised therein for the support of common schools. There are two points in the law that deserve consideration. First, the object of the fund was the aid and encouragement of the schools, and not their support; and secondly, the limit of appropriation to the respective towns was the amount raised by each. There is an apparent inconsistency in this restriction when it is considered that the income of the entire fund would have been equal to only forty-three cents for each child in the state between the ages of five and fifteen years, and that each town raised, annually, by taxation, a larger sum; but this inconsistency is to be explained by the fact that the public sentiment, as indicated by resolves reported by the same committee for the appointment of commissioners on the subject, tended to a distribution of money among the towns according to their educational wants.

As early as 1828, the Committee on Education of the House of Representatives, in a Report made by Hon. W. B. Calhoun, declared, "That means should be devised for the establishment of a fund having in view not the *support*, but the *encouragement*, of the common schools, and the instruction of school teachers." This report was made in the month of January, and in February following the same committee say: "The establishment of a fund should look to the support of an institution for the instruction of school teachers in each county in the commonwealth, and to the distribution, annually, to all the towns, of such a sum for the benefit of the schools as shall simply operate as an encouragement to proportionate efforts on the part of the towns. A fund which should be so large as to suffice for the support of the whole school establishment of the state, as is the case in Connecticut, would, in the opinion of the committee, be rather detrimental than advantageous; it would only serve to draw off from the mass of the community that animating interest which will ever be found indispensable where a resolute feeling upon the subject is wished for or expected. Such a result is, in every sense, to be deprecated, and whatever may tend to it, even remotely, should be anxiously avoided. A fund which should admit of the distribution of one thousand dollars to any town which should raise three thousand dollars, in any manner within itself, or in that proportion, would operate as a strong incentive to high efforts ; and, if to this should be added the further requisition of a faithful return to the Legislature, annually, of the condition of the schools, the consequences could not be otherwise than decidedly favorable." This report was accompanied by a bill "for the establishment of the Massachusetts Literary Fund." The bill followed the report in regard to the proportionate amount of the income of the fund to be distributed to the several towns. This bill failed to become a law.

In January, 1833, the House of Representatives, under an order introduced by Mr. Marsh, of Dalton, appointed a committee "to consider the expediency of investing a portion of the proceeds of the sales of the lands of this commonwealth in a permanent fund, the interest of which should be annually applied, as the Legislature should from time to time direct, for the encouragement of common schools." The adoption of this order was the incipient measure that led to the establishment of the Massachusetts School Fund. On the twenty-third of the same month, Mr. Marsh submitted the report of the committee. The committee acted upon the expectation that all moneys then in the treasury derived from the sale of public lands, and the entire proceeds of all subsequent sales, were to be set apart as a fund for the encouragement of common schools ; but, as blanks were left in the bill reported, they seem not to have been sanguine of the liberality of the Legislature. The cash and notes on hand amounted to $234,418.32, and three and a half millions of acres of land unsold amounted, at the estimated price of forty cents per acre, to $1,400,000 more ; making together a fund with a capital of $1,634,418.32. The income was estimated at $98,065.09. It was also stated that there were 140,000 children in the state between the ages of five and fifteen years, and it was therefore expected that the income of the fund would permit a distribution to the towns of seventy cents for each child between the afore-named ages. This certainly was a liberal expectation, compared with the results that have been attained. The distributive share of each child has amounted to only about one-third of the sum then contemplated. The committee were careful to say, "It is not intended, in establishing a school fund, to relieve towns and parents from the principal expense of education; but to manifest our interest in, and to give direction, energy, and stability to, institutions essential to individual happiness and the public welfare." In conclusion, the committee make the following inquiries and suggestions:

"Should not our common schools be brought nearer to their constitutional guardians? Shall we not adopt measures which shall bind, in grateful alliance, the youth to the governors of the commonwealth? We consider the application, annually, of the interest of the proposed fund, as the establishment of a direct communication betwixt the Legislature and the schools; as each representative can carry home the bounty of the government, and bring back from the schools returns of gratitude and proficiency. They will then cheerfully render all such information as the Legislature may desire. A new spirit would animate the community, from which we might hope the most happy results. This endowment would give the schools consequence and character, and would correct and elevate the standard of education.

"Therefore, to preserve the purity, extend the usefulness, and perpetuate the benefits of intelligence, we recommend that a fund be constituted, and the distribution of the income so ordered as to open a direct and more certain intercourse with the schools; believing that by this measure their wants would be better understood and supplied, the advantages of education more highly appreciated and improved, and the blessings of wisdom, virtue, and knowledge, carried home to the fireside of every family, to the bosom of every child." The bill reported by this committee was read twice, and then, upon Mr. Marsh's motion, referred to the next Legislature.

In 1834, the bill from the files of the last General Court to establish the Massachusetts School Fund, and so much of the petition of the inhabitants of Seekonk as related to the same subject, were referred to the Committee on Education.

In the month of February, Hon. A. D. Foster, of

Worcester, chairman of the committee, made a report, and submitted a bill which was the basis of the law of March 31, 1834. The committee were sensible of the importance of establishing a fund for the encouragement of the common schools. These institutions were languishing for support, and in a great degree destitute of the public sympathy. There were no means of communication between the government and the schools, and in some sections towns and districts had set themselves resolutely against all interference by the state. In 1832, an effort was made to ascertain the amount raised for the support of schools. Returns were received from only ninety-nine towns, showing an annual average expenditure of one dollar and ninety-eight cents for each pupil.

The interest in this subject does not seem to have been confined to the Legislature, nor even to have originated there. The report of the committee contains an extract from a communication made by Rev. William C. Woodbridge, then editor of the *American Annals of Education and Instruction.* His views were adopted by the committee, and they corresponded with those which have been already quoted. The dangers of a large fund were presented, and the example of Connecticut, and some states of the West, where school funds had diminished rather than increased the public interest in education, was tendered as a warning against a too liberal appropriation of public money. On the other hand, Mr. Woodbridge claimed that the establishment of a fund which should encourage efforts rather than supply all wants, and, without sustaining the schools, give aid to the people in proportion to their own contributions, was a measure indispensable to the cause of education. He also referred to the experience of New Jersey, which had made a general appropriation to be paid to those towns that should contribute for the support of their own schools; but, such was the public indifference, that after many years the money was still in the treasury. Hence it was inferred that all these measures were ineffectual, and that mere taxation was, upon the whole, to be preferred to any imperfect system. But the example of New York was approved, where the distribution of a small sum, equal to about twenty cents for each pupil, had increased the public interest, and wrought what then seemed to be an effectual and permanent revolution in educational affairs. These facts and reasonings, say the committee, seem to be important and sound, and to result in this, — that no provision ought to be made which shall diminish the present amount of money raised by taxes for the schools, or the interest felt by the people in their prosperity; that a fund may be so used as satisfactorily to increase both — and that further information in regard to our schools is requisite to determine the best mode of doing this. These opinions are supported generally by the judgment of the present generation. Yet it is to be remarked, by way of partial dissent, that the public apathy in Connecticut and the states of the West was not in a great degree the effect of the funds, but was rather a coëxisting, independent fact. It ought not, therefore, to have been expected that the mere offer of money for educational purposes, while the people had no just idea of the importance of education or of the means by which it could be acquired, would lead them even to accept the proffered boon; and it certainly, in their judgment, furnished no reason for self-taxation. It is, however, no doubt true that the power of local taxation for the support of schools is in its exercise a means of provoking interest in education; and it is reasonable to assume that a public system of instruction will never be vigorous and efficient at all times and under all circumstances where the right of local taxation does not exist or is not exercised. When the entire expenditure is derived from the income of public funds, or obtained by a universal tax, and the proceeds distributed among the towns, parishes, or districts, there will often be general conditions of public sentiment unfavorable, if not hostile, to schools; and, there will always be found in any state, however small, local indifference and lethargy which render all gifts, donations, and distributions, comparatively valueless. The subject of self-taxation annually is important in connection with a system of free education. It is the experience of the states of this country that the people themselves are more generous in the use of this power than are their representatives ; and it is also true that when the power has been exercised by the people, there is usually more interest awakened in regard to modes of expenditure, and more zeal manifested in securing adequate returns. The private conversations and public debates often arouse an interest which would never have been manifested had the means of education been furnished by a fund, or been distributed as the proceeds of a general tax assessed by the government of the state.

I have no doubt that much of our success is due to the fact that in all the towns the question of taxation is annually submitted to the people. It is quite certain that the sum of our municipal appropriations never could have been increased from $387,124.17, in 1837, to $1,341,252.03, in 1858, without the influence of the statistical tables that are appended to the Annual Reports of the Board of Education ; and it is also true that the materials for these tables could not have been secured without the agency of the school fund. Our experience as a state confirms the wisdom of the reports of 1833 and 1834; and I unreservedly concur in the opinion that a fund ought not to be sufficient for the support of schools, but that such a fund is needed to give encouragement to the towns, to stimulate the people to make adequate local appropriations, to secure accurate and complete returns from the committees, and finally to provide means for training teachers, and for defraying the necessary expenses of the educational department. The law of 1834, establishing the school fund, was reënacted in the Revised Statutes (chap. 11, sects. 13 and 14). The Revised Statutes (chap. 23, sects. 62, 63, 64, 65, 66, and 67) also required that returns should be made, each year, from all the towns of the commonwealth, of the condition of the schools in various important particulars. The income of the fund was to be apportioned among the towns that had raised, the preceding year, the sum of one dollar by taxation for each pupil, and had complied with the laws in other respects; and it was to be distributed according to the number of persons in each between the ages of four and sixteen years. These provisions have since been frequently and variously modified; but at all times the state has imposed similar conditions upon the towns. By the statute of 1839, chapter 56, the income of the school fund was to be apportioned among those towns that had raised by taxation for the support of schools the sum of one dollar and twenty-five cents for each person between the ages of four and sixteen years; and, by the law of 1849, chapter 117, the income was to be apportioned among those towns which had raised by taxation the sum of one dollar and fifty cents for the education of each person between the ages of five and fifteen years. This provision is now in force. By an act of the Legislature, passed April 15th, 1846, it was provided that all sums of money which should thereafter be drawn from the treasury, for educational purposes, should be considered as a charge upon the moiety of the proceeds of the sales of the public lands set apart for the purpose of constituting a school fund. This provision continued in force until the reörganization of the fund, in 1854. By the law of that year (chap. 300), it was provided that one half of the annual income of the fund should be apportioned and distributed among the towns according to the then existing provisions of law, and that the educational expenses before referred to should be chargeable to and paid from the other half of the income of said fund. These provisions are now in force.

The limitation of the act of 1834, establishing the

fund, and of the Revised Statutes, was removed by the law of 1851, chapter 112, and the amount of the fund was then fixed at one million and five hundred thousand dollars. By the act of 1854 the principal was limited to two millions of dollars. The Constitutional Convention of 1853 had, with great unanimity, declared it to be the duty of the Legislature to provide for the increase of the school fund to the sum of two millions of dollars ; and, though the proposed constitution was rejected by the people, the provision concerning the fund was generally, if not universally, acceptable. Under these circumstances, the legislature of 1854 may be said to have acted in conformity to the known opinion and purpose of the state.

On the 1st of June, 1858, the principal of the fund was $1,522,898.41, including the sum of $1,843.68, added during the year preceding that date. In this statement no notice is taken of the rights of the school fund in the Western Railroad Loan Sinking Fund.

It may be observed that the committee of 1833 contemplated the establishment of a fund, with a capital of $1,634,418.32, and yet, after twenty-five years, the Massachusetts School Fund amounts to only $1,522,898.41. Its present means of increase are limited to the excess of one-half of the annual income over the current educational expenses. The increase for the year 1856–7 was $4,142.90; and for the year 1857–8, $1,843.68. With this resource only, and at this rate of increase, about one hundred and sixty years will be required for the augmentation of the capital to the maximum contemplated by existing laws. But the educational wants of the state are such that even this scanty supply must soon cease. It is then due to the magnitude of the proposition for the considerable and speedy increase of the school fund, that its necessity, if possible, or its utility, at least, should be satisfactorily demonstrated; and it is for this purpose that I have already presented a brief sketch of its history in connection with the legislation of the commonwealth, and that I now proceed to set forth its relations to the practical work of public instruction.

When the fund was instituted, public sentiment in regard to education was lethargic, if not retrograding. The mere fact of the action of the Legislature lent new importance to the cause of learning, inspired its advocates with additional zeal, gave efficiency to previous and subsequent legislation, and, as though there had been a new creation, evoked order out of chaos.

Previous to 1834 there was no trustworthy information concerning the schools of the state. The law of 1826, chapter 143, section 8, required each town to make a report to the Secretary of the Commonwealth, of the amount of money paid, the number of schools, the aggregate number of months that the schools of each city and town were kept, the number of male and female teachers, the whole number of pupils, the number of private schools and academies and the number of pupils therein, the amount of compensation paid to the instructors of private schools and academies, and the number of persons between the ages of fourteen and twenty-one years who were unable to read and write. The Legislature did not provide a penalty for neglect of this provision, nor does there seem to have been any just method of compelling obedience. The Secretary of the Commonwealth sent out blank forms of returns, and replies were received from two hundred and fourteen towns, while eighty-eight were entirely silent.

The returns received furnish a series of interesting facts for the year 1826. There were one thousand seven hundred and twenty-six district schools, supported at an expense of two hundred and twenty-six thousand two hundred and nineteen dollars and ninety cents ($226,219.90), while there were nine hundred and fifty-three academies and private schools maintained at a cost of $192,455.10. The whole number of children attending public schools was 117,186, and the number educated in private schools and academies was 25,083. The expense, therefore, was $7.67 per pupil in the private schools, and only $1.93 each in the public schools. These facts are indicative of the condition of public sentiment. About one-sixth of the children of the state were educated in academies and private schools, at a cost equal to about six-sevenths of the amount paid for the education of the remaining five-sixths, who attended the public schools. The returns also showed that there were 2,974 children between the ages of seven and fourteen years who did not attend school, and 530 persons over fourteen years of age who were unable to read and write. The incompleteness of these returns detracts from their value; but, as those towns where the greatest interest existed were more likely to respond to the call of the Legislature, it is probable that the actual condition of the whole state was below that of the two hundred and eighty-eight towns. The interest which the law of 1826 had called forth was temporary; and in March, 1832, the Committee on Education, to whom was referred an order with instructions to inquire into the expediency of providing a fund to furnish, in certain cases, common schools with apparatus, books, and such other aid as may be necessary to raise the standard of common school education, say that they desire more accurate knowledge than could then be obtained. The returns required by law were in many cases wholly neglected, and in others they were inaccurately made. In the year 1831 returns were received from only eighty-six towns. In order to obtain the desired information, a special movement was made by the Legislature. The report of the committee was printed in all the newspapers that published the laws of the commonwealth, and the Secretary was directed to prepare and present to the Legislature an abstract of the returns which should be received from the several towns for the year 1832. The result of this extraordinary effort was seen in returns from only ninety-nine of three hundred and five towns, and even a large part of these were confessedly inaccurate or incomplete. They present, however, some remarkable facts.

The following table, prepared from the returns of 1832, shows the relative standing and cost of public and private schools in a part of the principal towns. It appears that the towns named in the table were educating rather more than two-thirds of their children in the public schools, at an expense of $2.88 each, and nearly one-third in private schools, at a cost of $12.70 each, and that the total expenditure for public instruction was about thirty-six per cent. of the outlay for educational purposes.

TOWNS.	Amount paid for public instruction during the year.	Whole No. of Pupils in the Public Schools in the course of the yr.	Number of Academies and Private Schools.	Number of Pupils in Academies and Private Schools, and not attending Public Schools.	Estimated amount of compensation of Instructors of Academies and Private Schools.
Beverly, . . .	$1,800 00	580	28	490	$2,365 33
Bradford, . .	750 00	600	9	177	1,725 00
Danvers, . .	2,000 00	873	6	150	1,500 00
Marblehead, .	2,200 00	650	31	650	3,800 00
Cambridge, .	3,600 00	970	16	441	5,732 00
Medford, . .	1,200 00	284	6	151	2,372 00
Newton, . .	1,600 00	542	3	100	2,975 00
Amherst, . .	850 00	556	2	270	4,600 00
Springfield, .	3,600 00	1,957	4	300	2,500 00
Greenfield, .	633 75	216	2	65	1,400 00
Dorchester, .	2,599 00	613	15	124	1,800 00
Quincy, . . .	1,800 00	465	7	106	2,741 50
Roxbury, . .	4,450 00	836	12	313	8,218 00
New Bedford,	4,000 00	1,268	15	537	6,300 00
Hingham, . .	2,144 00	703	8	180	2,625 00
Provincetown,	584 32	450	4	140	800 00
Edgartown, .	450 00	350	10	100	2,700 00
Nantucket, .	2,633 40	882	50	1,084	10,795 00
18 Towns,	$36,894 47	12,795	228	5,378	$64,948 83

The evidence is sufficient that the public schools were in a deplorable and apparently hopeless condition.

The change that has been effected in the eighteen towns named may be seen by comparing the following table with the one already given. In 1832, 64 per cent. of the amount paid for education was expended in academies and private schools, while in 1858 only 24 per cent. was so expended. In the same period the amount raised for public schools increased from less than thirty-seven thousand dollars to more than two hundred and fifty-nine thousand dollars. At the first period, the attendance of pupils upon academies and private schools was nearly 30 per cent. of the whole number, while in 1858 it was only 8 per cent. The private schools of some of these towns were established recently, and are sustained in a degree by pupils who are not inhabitants of the state, but who have come among us for the purpose of enjoying the culture which our teachers and schools, private as well as public, are able to furnish. If, as seems probable, the number of foreign pupils was less in 1832 than in 1858, the decrease of pupils in private schools would be greater than is indicated by the tables. The cost of education, as it appears by this table, is rather more than thirty dollars per pupil in the private schools, and only eight dollars and forty-nine cents in the public schools. In the following table, Bradford includes Groveland, Danvers includes South Danvers, Springfield includes Chicopee, and Roxbury includes West Roxbury. This is rendered necessary for the purposes of comparison, as Groveland, South Danvers, Chicopee, and West Roxbury, have been incorporated since 1832.

TOWNS.	Amount paid for Public Schools in 1857–8, including tax, income of Surplus Revenue, and of State School Fund, when such income is appropriated for such schools, and exclusive of sums paid for school-houses.	Whole No. of pupils attending Public Schools in 1857–8 — the largest No. returned as in attendance during any one term.	Number of incorporated and unincorporated Academies and Private Schools returned in 1858.	Estimated attendance in Academies and Private Schools in 1857–8.	Estimated amount of tuition paid in Academies and Priv. Schools in 1857–8.
Beverly, . . .	$5,748 20	1,114	1	10	$100 00
Bradford, . .	2,416 47	513	2	84	1,720 00
Danvers, . .	14,829 52	2,066	1	40	360 00
Marblehead, . .	7,311 10	1,188	6	160	1,390 00
Cambridge, . .	37,420 86	4,710	14	400	15,000 00
Medford, . . .	7,794 44	837	5	130	3,800 00
Newton, . . .	12,263 50	1,138	8	308	22,800 00
Amherst, . . .	2,142 80	536	5	121	3,934 00
Springfield, . .	27,324 84	3,864	6	–	–
Greenfield, . .	2,627 50	589	2	25	1,800 00
Dorchester, . .	22,338 51	1,795	1	31	600 00
Quincy, ...	8,861 46	1,260	2	20	225 00
Roxbury, . .	50,000 00	4,400	25	561	10,600 00
New Bedford, .	36,074 25	3,548	20	434	15,074 00
Hingham, . . .	4,904 13	728	2	71	1,717 56
Provincetown, .	3,147 26	689	–	–	–
Edgartown, . .	2,578 63	380	8	96	200 00
Nantucket, . .	11,596 27	1,198	13	259	3,466 23
Totals, . . .	$259,379 74	30,553	121	2,750	$82,786 79

The Legislature of 1834 acted with wisdom and energy. The school fund having been established, the towns were next required to furnish answers to certain questions that were substituted for the requisition of the statute of 1826, and any town whose committee failed to make the return was to be deprived of its share of the income of the school fund, whenever it should be first distributed. (Res. 1834, chap. 78.)

Those measures were in the highest degree salutary. There were 305 towns in the state, and returns were received from 261. There was still a want of accuracy and completeness; but from this time forth the state secured what had never before been attained, — intelligent legislation by the government, and intelligent coöperation and support by the people.

In December, 1834, the Secretary of the Commonwealth prepared an aggregate of the returns received, of which the following is a copy:

Number of towns from which returns have been received, .	261
Number of school districts, ...	2,251
Number of male children attending school from four to sixteen years of age, ...	67,499
Number of female children attending school from four to sixteen years of age, ...	63,728
Number over sixteen and under twenty-one unable to read and write, ...	158
Number of male instructors, ...	1,967
Number of female instructors, ...	2,388
Amount raised by tax to support schools, ...	$310,178 87
Amount raised by contribution to support schools, . .	15,141 25
Average number of scholars attending academies and private schools, ...	24,749

Estimated amount paid for tuition in academies and private schools, ... $276,575 75
Local funds — Yes, ... 71
Local funds — No, ... 181

Thus, by the institution of the school fund, provision was made for a system of annual returns, from which has been drawn a series of statistical tables, that have not only exhibited the school system as a whole and in its parts, but have also contributed essentially to its improvement.

These statistics have been so accurate and complete, for many years, as to furnish a safe basis for legislation ; and they have at the same time been employed by the friends of education as means for awakening local interest, and stimulating and encouraging the people to assume freely and bear willingly the burdens of taxation. It is now easy for each town, or for any inhabitant, to know what has been done in any other town ; and, as a consequence, those that do best are a continual example to those that, under ordinary circumstances, might be indifferent. The establishment and efficiency of the school-committee system is due also to the same agency. There are, I fear, some towns that would now neglect to choose a school committee, were there not a small annual distribution of money by the state ; but, in 1832, the duty was often either neglected altogether, or performed in such a manner that no appreciable benefit was produced. The superintending committee is the most important agency connected with our system of instruction. In some portions of the state the committees are wholly, and in others they are partly, responsible for the qualifications of teachers ; they everywhere superintend and give character to the schools, and by their annual reports they exert a large influence over public opinion. The people now usually elect well-qualified men ; and it is believed that the extracts from the local reports, published annually by the Board of Education, constitute the best series of papers in the language upon the various topics that have from time to time been considered.* By the publication

* An eminent friend of education, and an Englishman, speaking of the reports for the year 1856–7, says : "The views enunciated by your local committees, while they have the sobriety indicative of practical knowledge, are at the same time enlightened and expansive. The writers of such reports must be of inestimable aid to your schoolmasters, standing as they do between the teacher and the parent, and exercising the most wholesome influence on both. Let me remark, in passing, that I am struck with the power of composition evinced in these provincial papers. Clear exposition, great command of the best English, correctness and even elegance of style, are their characteristics."

of these abstracts, the committees, and indeed the people generally, are made acquainted with everything that has been done, or is at any time doing, in the commonwealth. Improvements that would otherwise remain local are made universal; information in regard to general errors is easily communicated, and the errors themselves are speedily removed, while the system is, in all respects, rendered homogeneous and efficient.

Nor does it seem to be any disparagement of Massachusetts to assume that, in some degree, she is indebted to the school fund for the consistent and steady policy of the Legislature, pursued for more than twenty years, and executed by the agency of the Board of Education. In this period, normal schools have been established, which have educated a large number of teachers, and exerted a powerful and ever increasing influence in favor of good learning. Teachers' Institutes have been authorized, and the experiment successfully tested. Agents of the Board of Education have been appointed, so that it is now possible, by the aid of both these means, as is shown by accompanying returns and statements, to afford, each year, to the people of a majority of the towns an opportunity to confer with those who are specially devoted to the work of education. In all this period of time, the Legislature has never been called upon to provide money for the expenses which have thus been incurred ; and, though a rigid scrutiny has been exercised over the expenditures of the educational department, measures for the promotion of the common schools have never been considered in relation to the general finances of the commonwealth. While some states have hesitated, and others have vacillated, Massachusetts has had a consistent, uniform, progressive policy, which is due in part to the consideration already named, and in part, no doubt, to a popular opinion, traditional and historical in its origin, but sustained and strengthened by the measures and experience of the last quarter of a century, that a system of public instruction is so important an element of general prosperity as to justify all needful appropriations for its support.

It may, then, be claimed for the Massachusetts School Fund, that the expectations of those by whom it was established have been realized ; that it has given unity and efficiency to the school system ; that it has secured accurate and complete returns from all the towns ; that it has, consequently, promoted a good understanding between the Legislature and the people ; that it has increased local taxation, but has never been a substitute for it ; and that it has enabled the Legislature, at all times and in every condition of the general finances, to act with freedom in regard to those agencies which are deemed essential to the prosperity of the common schools of the state.

Having thus, in the history of the school fund, fully justified its establishment, so in its history we find sufficient reasons for its sacred preservation. While other communities, and even other states, have treated educational funds as ordinary revenue, subject only to an obligation on the part of the public to bestow an annual income on the specified object, Massachusetts has ever acted in a fiduciary relation, and considered herself responsible for the principal as well as the income of the fund, not only to this generation, but to every generation that shall occupy the soil, and inherit the name and fame of this commonwealth.

It only remains for me to present the reasons which render an increase of the capital of the fund desirable, if not necessary. The annual income of the existing fund amounts to about ninety-three thousand dollars, one-half of which is distributed among the towns and cities, in proportion to the number of persons in each between the ages of five and fifteen years. The distribution for the year 1857–8 amounted to twenty cents and eight mills for each child. The following table shows the annual distribution to the towns from the year 1836; the whole number of children for each year except 1836 and 1840, when the entire population was the basis; and the amount paid on account of each child since the year 1849, when the law establishing the present method of distribution was enacted:

Year.	Children.	Income.	Income per pupil.	Year.	Children.	Income.	Per Pupil in Cents & Mills.
1836.	473,684	$16,230 57*	–	1848.	210,403	$33,874 87	–
1837.	160,676	19,002 74†	–	1849.	210,770	33,723 20	–
1838.	174,984	19,970 47	–	1850.	182,003	37,370 51‖	.205
1839.	180,070	21,358 81	–	1851.	192,849	41,462 54	.215
1840.	701,331	21,202 64‡	–	1852.	198,050	44,066 12	.222
1841.	179,967	32,109 32§	–	1853.	199,292	46,908 10	.235
1842.	179,917	24,006 89	–	1854.	202,102	48,504 48	.240
1843.	173,416	24,094 87	–	1855.	210,761	46,788 94	.222
1844.	158,193	22,932 71	–	1856.	221,902	44,842 75	.202
1845.	170,823	28,248 35	–	1857.	220,336	46,783 64	.212
1846.	195,032	30,150 27	–	1858.	222,860	46,496 19	.208
1847.	197,475	34,511 89	–				

* Distributed among the cities and towns, according to an Act of 1835. (Stat. 138, § 2.)

† Distributed among the cities and towns, according to the number of persons in each between the ages of four and sixteen years. (Rev. Stat., chap. 23, § 67.)

‡ Income distributed among the cities and towns, according to population, under an Act passed Feb. 22, 1840. (Stat. 1840, chap. 7.) This act was re pealed by an act passed Feb. 8, 1841. (Stat. 1841, chap. 17, § 2.)

§ Distributed among the cities and towns, according to the number of persons in each between the ages of four and sixteen years. (Stat. 1841, chap. 17, § 2.)

‖ Distributed among the cities and towns, according to the number of persons in each between the ages of five and fifteen years. (Stat. 1849, chap. 117, § 2.)

It was contemplated by the founders of the school fund that an amount might safely be distributed among the towns equal to one-third of the sums raised by taxation, but the state is really furnishing only one-thirtieth of the annual expenditure. A distribution corresponding to the original expectation is neither desirable nor possible ; but a substantial addition might be made without in any degree diminishing the interest of the people, or relieving them from taxation. The income of the school fund has been three times used as a means of increasing the appropriations in the towns. It is doubtful whether, without an addition to the fund, this power can be again applied ; and yet there are, according to the last returns, twenty-two towns that do not raise a sum for schools equal to $2.50 for each child between the ages of five and fifteen years ; and there are fifty-two towns whose appropriations are less than three dollars. When the average annual expenditure is over six dollars, the minimum ought not to be less than three.

It is to be considered that, as population increases, the annual personal distribution will diminish, and consequently that the bond now existing between the Legislature and people will be weakened. Moreover, any definite sum of money is worth less than it was twenty years ago ; and it is reasonably certain that the same sum will be less valuable in 1860, and yet less valuable in 1870, than it is now. Hence, if the fund remain nominally the same, it yet suffers a practical annual decrease. It is further to be presumed that the Legislature will find it expedient to advance in its legislation from year to year. A small number of towns, few or many, may not always approve of what is done, and it is quite important that the influence of the fund should be sufficient to enable the state to execute its policy with uniformity and precision.

As is well known, the expenses of the educational department are defrayed from the other half of the income of the fund. From this income the forty-eight scholarships in the colleges, the Normal Schools, the Teachers' Institutes, the Agents of the Board of Education, are supported, and the salaries of the Secretary and the Assistant-Secretary are paid. As has been stated, the surplus carried to the capital of the fund in June last was only $1,843.68. The objects of expenditure, already named, may be abolished, but no reasonable plan of economy can effect much saving while they exist. It is also reasonably certain that the expenses of the department must be increased. The law now provides for twelve Teachers' Institutes, annually, and there were opportunities during the present year for holding them ; but, in order that one agent might be constantly employed, and a second employed for the term of six months, I limited the number of sessions to ten.

The salaries of the teachers in the Normal Schools are low, and the number of persons employed barely adequate to the work to be done. Some change, involving additional expense, is likely to be called for in the course of a few years.

In view of the eminent aid which the school fund has rendered to the cause of education, with due deference to the wisdom and opinions of its founders, and with just regard to the existing and probable necessities of the state in connection with the cause of education, I earnestly favor the increase of the school fund by the addition of a million and a half of dollars.

Nor does the proposition for the state to appropriate annually $180,000 in aid of the common schools seem unreasonable, when it is considered that the military expenses are $65,000, the reformatory and correctional about $200,000, the charitable about $45,000, and the pauper expenses nearly $250,000 more, all of which will diminish as our schools are year by year better qualified to give thorough and careful intellectual, moral, and religious culture.

This increase seems to be necessary in order that the Massachusetts School Fund may furnish aid to the common schools during the next quarter of a century proportionate to the relative influence exerted by the same agency during the last twenty-five years. Nor will such an addition give occasion for any apprehension that the zeal of the people will be diminished in the least. Were there to be no increase of population in the state, the distribution for each pupil would never exceed forty cents, or about one-fifteenth of the amount now raised by taxation.

So convinced are the people of Massachusetts of the importance of common schools, and so much are they accustomed to taxation for their support, that there is no occasion to hesitate, lest we should follow the example of those communities where large funds, operating upon an uneducated and inexperienced popular opinion, have injured rather than benefited the public schools. The ancient policy of the commonwealth will be continued ; but, whenever the people see the government, by solemn act, manifesting its confidence in schools and learning, they will be encouraged to guard and sustain the institutions of the fathers.

A SYSTEM OF AGRICULTURAL EDUCATION.

[An Address before the Barnstable Agricultural Society, Oct. 8, 1857.]

In the month of February, 1855, a distinguished American, who has read much, and acquired, by conversation, observation, and travels in this country and Europe, the highest culture of American society, wrote these noticeable sentences: "The farmers have not kept pace, in intelligence, with the rest of the community. They do not put brain-manure enough into their acres. Our style of farming is slovenly, dawdling, and stupid, and the waste, especially in manure, is immense. I suppose we are about, in farming, where the Lowlands of Scotland were fifty years ago; and what immense strides agriculture has made in Great Britain since the battle of Waterloo, and how impossible it would have been for the farmers to have held their own without!" *

It would not be civil for me to endorse these statements as introductory to a brief address upon Agricultural Education; but I should not accept them at

* Hon. George S. Hillard.

all did they not contain truth enough to furnish a text for a layman's discourse before an assembly of farmers.

Competent American travellers concur in the opinion that the Europeans generally, and especially our brethren of England, Ireland, and Scotland, are far in advance of us in scientific and practical agriculture. This has been stated or admitted by Mr. Colman, President Hitchcock, and last by Mr. French, who has recently visited Europe under the auspices of the National Agricultural Society.

There are good reasons for the past and for the existing superiority of the Old World ; and there are good reasons, also, why this superiority should not much longer continue. Europe is old, — America is young. Land has been cultivated for centuries in Europe, and often by the same family ; its capacity tested, its fitness or unfitness for particular crops proved, the local and special effects of different fertilizers well known, and the experience of many generations has been preserved, so as to be equivalent to a like experience, in time and extent, by the present occupants of the soil.

In America there are no family estates, nor long occupation by the same family of the same spot. Cultivated lands have changed hands as often as every twenty-five years from the settlement of the country. The capacity of our soils to produce, when laboriously and systematically cultivated, has not been ascertained; there has been no accumulation of experience by families, and but little by the public; and the effort, in many sections, has been to draw as much as possible from the land, while little or nothing was returned to it. Farming, as a whole, has not been a system of cultivation, which implies improvement, but a process of exhaustion. It has been easier for the farmer, though, perhaps, not as economical, if all the elements necessary to a correct opinion could be combined, to exchange his worn-out lands for fresh soils, than to adopt an improving system of agriculture. The present has been consulted; the future has been disregarded. As the half-civilized hunters of the pampas of Buenos Ayres make indiscriminate slaughter of the myriads of wild cattle that roam over the unfenced prairies of the south, and preserve the hides only for the commerce and comfort of the world, so we have clutched from nature whatever was in sight or next at hand, regardless of the actual and ultimate wrong to physical and vegetable life; and, as the pioneers of a better civilization now gather up the bones long neglected and bleaching under tropical suns and tropical rains, and by the agency of trade, art, and industry, extort more wealth from them than was originally derived from the living animals, so we shall find that worn-out lands, when subjected to skilful, careful, scientific husbandry, are quite as profitable as the virgin soils, which, from the day of the migration into the Connecticut valley to the occupancy of the Missouri and the Kansas, have proved so tempting to our ancestors and to us. But there has been some philosophy, some justice, and considerable necessity, in the course that has been pursued. Subsistence is the first desire; and, in new countries where forests are to be felled, dwellings erected, public institutions established, roads and bridges built, settlers cannot be expected, in the cultivation of the land, to look much beyond the present moment. And they are entitled to the original fertility of the soil. Europe passed through the process of settlement and exhaustion many centuries ago. Her recovery has been the work of centuries, — ours may be accomplished in a few years, even within the limits of a single life. The fact from which an improving system of agriculture must proceed is apparent in the northern and central Atlantic states, and is, in a measure, appreciated in the West. We have all heard that certain soils were inexhaustible. The statement was first made of the valley of the Connecticut, then of the Genesee country, then of Ohio, then of Illinois, and occasionally we now hear similar statements of Kansas, or California, or the valley of the Willamette. In the nature of things these statements were erroneous. The idea of soil, in reason and in the use of the word, contains the idea of exhaustion. Soil is not merely the upper stratum of the earth ; it is a substance which possesses the power, under certain circumstances, of giving up essential properties of its own for the support of vegetable and ultimately of animal life. What it gives up it loses, and to the extent of its loss it is exhausted. It is no more untrue to say that the great cities of the world have not, in their building, exhausted the forests and the mines to any extent, than to say that the annual abundant harvests of corn and wheat have not, in any degree, exhausted the prairies and bottom lands of the West. Some lands may be exhausted for particular crops in a single year ; others in five years, others in ten, while others may yield undiminished returns for twenty, fifty, or even a hundred years. But it is plain that annual cropping without rotation, and without compensation by nature or art, must finally deprive the soil of the required elements. Nor should we deceive ourselves by considering only those exceptions whose existence is due to the fact that nature makes compensation for the loss. Annual or occasional irrigation with rich deposits, — as upon the Nile and the Connecticut, — allowing the land to lie fallow, rotation of crops and the growth of wood, are so many expedients and provisions by which nature increases the productiveness of the earth. Nor is a great depth of soil, as two, five, ten, or twenty feet, any security against its ultimate impoverishment. Only a certain portion is available. It has been found in the case of coal-mines which lie at great depths, that they are, for the present, valueless; and we cannot attach much importance to soil that is twenty feet below the surface. Neither cultivation nor vegetation can go beyond a certain depth; and wherever vegetable life exists, its elements are required and appropriated. Great depth of soil is desirable; but, with our present knowledge and means of culture, it furnishes no security against ultimate exhaustion.

The fact that all soils are exhaustible establishes the necessity for agricultural education, by whose aid the processes of impoverishment may be limited in number and diminished in force; and the realization of this fact by the public generally is the only justification necessary for those who advocate the immediate application of means to the proposed end.

And, gentlemen, if you will allow a festive day to be marred by a single word of criticism, I feel constrained to say, that a great obstacle to the increased usefulness, further elevation, and higher respectability, of agriculture, is in the body of farmers themselves. And I assume this to be so upon the supposition that agriculture is not a cherished pursuit in many farmers' homes; that the head of the family often regards his life of labor upon the land as a necessity from which he would willingly escape; that he esteems other pursuits as at once less laborious, more profitable, and more honorable, than his own; that children, both sons and daughters, under the influence of parents, both father and mother, receive an education at home, which neither school, college, nor newspaper, can counteract, that leads them to abandon the land for the store, the shop, the warehouse, the professions, or the sea.

The reasonable hope of establishing a successful system of agricultural education is not great where such notions prevail.

Agriculture is not to attain to true practical dignity by the borrowed lustre that eminent names, ancient and modern, may have lent to it, any more than the earth itself is warmed and made fruitful by the aurora borealis of an autumn night. Our system of public instruction, from the primary school to the college, rests mainly upon the public belief in its importance, its possibility, and its necessity. It is easy on a professional holiday to believe in the respectability of agriculture; but is it a living sentiment, controlling your conduct, and inspiring you with courage and faith in your daily labor? Does it lead you to contemplate with satisfaction the prospect that your son is to be a farmer also, and that your daughter is to be a farmer's wife? These, I imagine, are test questions which not all farmers nor farmers' wives can answer in the affirmative. Else, why the custom among farmers' sons of making their escape, at the earliest moment possible, from the labors and restraints of the farm? Else, why the disposition of the farmer's daughter to accept other situations, not more honorable, and in the end not usually more profitable, than the place of household aid to the business of the home? How, then, can a system of education be prosperous and efficient, when those for whom it is designed neither respect their calling nor desire to pursue it? You will not, of course, imagine that I refer, in these statements, to all farmers; there are many exceptions; but my own experience and observation lead me to place confidence in the fitness of these remarks, speaking generally of the farmers of New England. It is, however, true, and the statement of the truth ought not to be omitted, that the prevalent ideas among us are much in advance of what they were ten years ago. In what has been accomplished we have ground for hope, and even security for further advancement.

I look, then, first and chiefly to an improved home culture, as the necessary basis of a system of agricultural education. Christian education, culture, and life, depend essentially upon the influences of home; and we feel continually the importance of kindred influences upon our common school system.

It will not, of course, be wise to wait, in the establishment of a system of agricultural education, until we are satisfied that every farmer is prepared for it; in the beginning sufficient support may be derived from a small number of persons, but in the end it must be sustained by the mass of those interested. Other pursuits and professions must meet the special claims made upon them, and in the matter of agricultural education they cannot be expected to do more than assent to what the farmers themselves may require.

An important part of a system of agricultural education has been, as it seems to me, already established. I speak of our national, state, county, and town associations for the promotion of agriculture. The first three may educate the people through their annual fairs, by their publications, and by the collection and distribution of rare seeds, plants, and animals, that are not usually within reach of individual farmers. By such means, and others less noticeable, these agencies can exert a powerful influence upon the farmers of the country; but their thorough, systematic education must be carried on at home. And for local and domestic education I think we must rely upon our public schools, upon town clubs or associations of farmers, and upon scientific men who may be appointed by the government to visit the towns, confer with the people, and receive and communicate information upon the agricultural resources and defects of the various localities. It will be observed that in this outline of a plan of education I omit the agricultural college. This omission is intentional, and I will state my reasons for it. I speak, however, of the present; the time may come when such an institution will be needed. In Massachusetts, Mr. Benjamin Bussey has made provision for a college at Roxbury, and Mr. Oliver Smith has made similar provision for a college at Northampton; but these bequests will not be available for many years. In England, Ireland, Scotland, France, Belgium, Prussia, Russia, Austria, and the smaller states of Europe, agricultural schools and colleges have been established; and they appear to be the most numerous where the ignorance of the people is the greatest. England has five colleges and schools, Ireland sixty-three, while Scotland has only a professorship in each of her colleges at Aberdeen and Edinburgh. In France, there are seventy-five agricultural schools ; but in seventy of them — called inferior schools — the instruction is a compound of that given in our public schools and the discipline of a good farmer upon his land, with some special attention to agricultural reading and farm accounts. Such schools are not desired and would not be patronized among us. When an agricultural school is established, it must be of a higher grade, — it must take rank with the colleges of the country. President Hitchcock, in his report, published in 1851, states that six professors would be required ; that the first outlay would be sixty-seven thousand dollars, and that the annual expense would be six thousand and two hundred dollars. By these arrangements and expenditures he contemplates the education of one hundred students, who are to pay annually each for tuition the sum of forty dollars. It was also proposed to connect an agricultural department with several of the existing academies, at an annual expense of three thousand dollars more. These estimates of cost seem low, nor do I find in this particular any special objection to the recommendation made by the commissioners of the government; any other scheme is likely to be quite as expensive in the end.

My chief objection is, that such a plan is not comprehensive enough, and cannot, in a reasonable time, sensibly affect the average standard of agricultural learning among us. The graduation of fifty students a year would be equal to one in a thousand or fifteen hundred of the farmers of the state; and in ten years there would not be one professionally educated farmer in a hundred. We are not, of course, to overlook the indirect influence of such a school, through its students annually sent forth: the better modes of culture adopted by them would, to some extent, be copied by others; nor are we to overlook the probability of a prejudice against the institution and its graduates, growing out of the republican ideas of equality prevailing among us. But the struggle against mere prejudice would be an honorable struggle, if, in the hour of victory, the college could claim to have reformed and elevated materially the practices and ideas of the farmers of the country. I fear that even victory under such circumstances would not be complete success. An institution established in New England must look to the existing peculiarities of our country, rather than venture at once upon the adoption of schemes that may have been successful elsewhere. Here every farmer is a laborer himself, employing usually from one to three hands, and they are often persons who look to the purchase and cultivation of a farm on their own account; while in England the master farmer is an overseer rather than a laborer. The number of men in Europe who own land or work it on their own account is small; the number of laborers whose labors are directed by the proprietors and farmers is quite large. Under these circumstances, if the few are educated, the work will go successfully on; while here, our agricultural education ought to reach the great body of those who labor upon the land. Will a college in each state answer the demand for agricultural education now existing? Is it safe in any country, or in any profession or pursuit, to educate a few, and leave the majority to the indirect influence of the culture thus bestowed? And is it philosophical, in this country, where there is a degree of personal and professional freedom such as is nowhere else enjoyed, to found a college or higher institution of learning upon the general and admitted ignorance of the people in the given department? or is it wiser, by elementary training and the universal diffusion of better ideas, to make the establishment of the college the necessity of the culture previously given? Every new school, not a college, makes the demand for the college course greater than it was before; and the advance made in our public schools increases the students in the colleges and the university. We build from the primary school to the college; and without the primary school and its dependents, — the grammar, high school, and academy, — the colleges would cease to exist. This view of education supports the statement that an agricultural college is not the foundation of a system of agricultural training, but a result that is to be reached through a preliminary and elementary course of instruction. What shall that course be? I say, first, the establishment of town or neighborhood societies of farmers and others interested in agriculture. These societies ought to be auxiliary to the county societies, and they never can become their rivals or enemies unless they are grossly perverted in their management and purposes. As such societies must be mutual and voluntary in their character, they can be established in any town where there are twenty, ten, or even five persons who are disposed to unite together. Its object would, of course, be the advancement of practical agriculture; and it would look to theories and even to science as means only for the attainment of a specified end. The exercises of such societies would vary according to the tastes and plans of the members and directors; but they would naturally provide for discussions and conversations among themselves, lectures from competent persons, the establishment of a library, and for the collection of models and drawings of domestic animals, models of varieties of fruit, specimens of seeds, grasses, and grains, rocks, minerals, and soils. The discussions and conversations would be based upon the actual observation and experience of the members; and agriculture would at once become better understood and more carefully practised by each person who intended to contribute to the exercises of the meeting.

Until the establishment of agricultural journals, there were no means by which the results of individual experience could be made known to the mass of farmers; and, even now, men of the largest experience are not the chief contributors.

Wherever a local club exists, it is always possible to compare the knowledge of the different members; and the results of such comparison may, when deemed desirable, be laid before the public at large. It is also in the power of such an organization thoroughly and at once to test any given experiment. The attention of this section of the country has been directed to the culture of the Chinese sugar-cane; and merchants, economists, and statesmen, as well as the farmers themselves, are interested in the speedy and satisfactory solution of so important an industrial problem. Had the attention of a few local societies in different parts of New England been directed to the culture, with special reference to its feasibility and profitableness, a definite result might have been reached the present year. The growth of flax, both in the means of cultivation and in economy, is a subject of great importance. Many other crops might also be named, concerning which opposite, not to say vague, opinions prevail. The local societies may make these trials through the agency of individual members better than they can be made by county and state societies, and better than they can usually be made upon model or experimental farms. It will often happen upon experimental farms that the circumstances do not correspond to the condition of things among the farmers. The combined practical wisdom of such associations must be very great; and I have but to refer to the published minutes of the proceedings of the Concord Club to justify this statement in its broadest sense. The meetings of such a club have all the characteristics of a school of the highest order. Each member is at the same time a teacher and a pupil. The meeting is to the farmer what the court-room is to the lawyer, the hospital to the physician, and the legislative assembly to the statesman.

Moot courts alone will not make skilful lawyers; the manikin is but an indifferent teacher of anatomy; and we may safely say that no statesman was ever made so by books, schools, and street discussions, without actual experience in some department of government.

It is, of course, to be expected that an agricultural college would have the means of making experiments; but each experiment could be made only under a single set of circumstances, while the agency of local societies, in connection with other parts of the plan that I have the honor diffidently to present, would convert at once a county or a state into an experimental farm for a given time and a given purpose. The local club being always practical and never theoretical, dealing with things always and never with signs, presenting only facts and never conjectures, would, as a school for the young farmer, be quite equal, and in some respects superior, to any that the government can establish. But, it may be asked, will you call that a school which is merely an assembly of adults without a teacher? I answer that technically it is not a school, but that in reality such an association is a school in the best use of the word. A school is, first, for the development of powers and qualities whose germs already exist; then for the acquisition of knowledge previously possessed by others; then for the prosecution of original inquiries and investigations. The associations of which I speak would possess all these powers, and contemplate all these results; but that their powers might be more efficient, and for the advancement of agriculture generally, it seems to me fit and proper for the state to appoint scientific and practical men as agents of the Board of Agriculture, and lecturers upon agricultural science and labor. If an agricultural college were founded, a farm would be required, and at least six professors would be necessary. Instead of a single farm, with a hundred young men upon it, accept gratuitously, as you would no doubt have opportunity, the use of many farms for experiments and repeated trials of crops, and, at the same time, educate, not a hundred only, but many thousand young men, nearly as well in theory and science, and much better in practical labor, than they could be educated in a college. Six professors, as agents, could accomplish a large amount of necessary work; possibly, for the present, all that would be desired. Assume, for this inquiry, that Massachusetts contains three hundred agricultural towns; divide these towns into sections of fifty each; then assign one section to each agent, with the understanding that his work for the year is to be performed in that section, and then that he is to be transferred to another. By a rotation of appointments and a succession of labors, the varied attainments of the lecturers would be enjoyed by the whole commonwealth. But, it may be asked, what, specifically stated, shall the work of the agents be? Only suggestions can be offered in answer to this inquiry. An agent might, in the summer season, visit his fifty towns, and spend two days in each. While there, he could ascertain the kinds of crops, modes of culture, nature of soils, practical excellences, and practical defects, of the farmers; and he might also provide for such experiments as he desired to have made. It would, likewise, be in his power to give valuable advice, where it might be needed, in regard to farming proper, and also to the erection and repair of farm-buildings. I am satisfied that a competent agent would, in this last particular alone, save to the people a sum equal to the entire cost of his services. After this labor was accomplished, eight months would remain for the preparation and delivery of lectures in the fifty towns previously visited. These lectures might be delivered in each town, or the agent might hold meetings of the nature of institutes in a number of towns centrally situated. In either case, the lectures would be at once scientific and practical; and their practical character would be appreciated in the fact that a judicious agent would adapt his lectures to the existing state of things in the given locality. This could not be done by a college, however favorably situated, and however well accomplished in the material of education. It is probable that the lectures would be less scientific than those that would be given in a college; but when their superior practical character is considered, and when we consider also that they would be listened to by the great body of farmers, old and young, while those of the college could be enjoyed by a small number of youth only, we cannot doubt which would be the most beneficial to the state, and to the cause of agriculture in the country.

An objection to the plan I have indicated may be found in the belief that the average education of the farmers is not equal to a full appreciation of the topics and lectures to be presented. My answer is, that the lecturers must meet the popular intelligence, whatever it is. Nothing is to be assumed by the teacher; it is his first duty to ascertain the qualifications of his pupils. I am, however, led to the opinion that the schools of the country have already laid a very good basis for practical instruction in agriculture; and, if this be not so, then an additional argument will be offered for the most rapid advance possible in our systems of education. In any event, it is true that the public schools furnish a large part of the intellectual culture given in the inferior and intermediate agricultural schools of Europe.

The great defect in the plan I have presented is this: That no means are provided for the thorough education needed by those persons who are to be appointed agents, and no provision is made for testing the qualities of soils, and the elements of grains, grasses, and fruits. My answer to this suggestion is, that it is in part, at least, well founded; but that the scientific schools furnish a course of study in the natural sciences which must be satisfactory to the best educated farmer or professor of agricultural learning, and that analyses may be made in the laboratories of existing institutions.

It is my fortune to be able to read a letter from Professor Horsford, which furnishes a satisfactory view of the ability of the Scientific School at Cambridge.

"*Cambridge, Sept.* 19, 1857.

"MY DEAR SIR: The occupation incident to the opening of the term has prevented an earlier answer to your letter of inquiry in regard to the Scientific School.

"The Scientific School furnishes, I believe, the necessary scientific knowledge for students of agriculture (such as you mention), 'who have been well educated at our high schools, academies, or colleges, and have also been trained practically in the business of farming.' It provides:

"1st. Practical instruction in the modes of experimental investigation. This is, I know, an unrecognized department, but it is, perhaps, the better suited name to the course of instruction of our chemical department. It qualifies the student for the most direct methods of solving the practical problems which are constantly arising in practical agriculture. It includes the analysis of soils, the manufacture and testing of manures, the philosophy of improved methods of culture, of rotation of crops, of dairy production, of preserving fruits, meats, &c. It applies more or less directly to the whole subject of mechanical expedients.

"2d. Practical instruction in surveying, mensuration, and drawing.

"3d. And by lectures — in botany, geology, zoology, comparative anatomy, and natural philosophy.

"Some of them — indeed, all of them, if desired — might be pursued practically, and with the use of apparatus and specimens.

"This course contemplates a period of study of from one year to two and a half years, according to the qualification of the pupil at the outset. He appears an hour each day at the blackboard, where he shares the drill of a class, and where he acquires a facility of illustration, command of language, an address and thorough consciousness of real knowledge, which are of more value, in many cases, as you know, than almost any amount of simple acquisition. He also attends, on an average, about one lecture a day throughout the year. During the remaining time he is occupied with experimental work in the laboratory or field.

"The great difficulty with students of agriculture, who might care to come to the Scientific School, is the expense of living in Cambridge. If some farmer at a distance of three or four miles from college, where rents for rooms are low, would open a boarding-house for students of agriculture in the Scientific School, where the care of a kitchen garden and some stock might be intrusted to them, and where a farmer's plain table might be spread at the price at which laborers would be received, we might hope that our facilities would be taken advantage of on a larger scale. As it is, but few, comparatively, among our students, come to qualify themselves for farming."

I should, however, consider the arrangements proposed as temporary, and finally to be abandoned or made permanent, as experience should dictate.

It may be said, I think, without disparagement to the many distinguished and disinterested men who have labored for the advancement of agriculture, that the operations of the government and of the state and county societies have no plan or system by which, as a whole, they are guided. The county societies have been and are the chief means of influence and progress ; but they have no power which can be systematically applied ; their movements are variable, and their annual exhibitions do not always indicate the condition of agriculture in the districts represented. They have become, to a certain extent, localized in the vicinity of the towns where the fairs are held ; and yet they do not possess the vigor which institutions positively local would enjoy.

The town clubs hold annual fairs ; and these fairs should be made tributary, in their products and in the interest they excite, to the county fairs. Let the town fairs be held as early in the season as practicable, and then let each town send to the county fairs its first-class premium articles as the contributions of the local society, as well as of the individual producers. Thus a healthful and generous rivalry would be stirred up between the towns of a county as well as among the citizens of each town ; and a county exhibition upon the plan suggested would represent at one view the general condition of agriculture in the vicinity. No one can pretend that this is accomplished by the present arrangements. Moreover, the county society, in its management and in its annual exhibitions, would possess an importance which it had not before enjoyed. As each town would be represented by the products of the dairy, the herd, and the field, so it would be represented by its men ; and the annual fair of the county would be a truthful and complete exposition of its industrial standing and power.

Out of a system thus broad, popular, and strong, an agricultural college will certainly spring, if such an institution shall be needed. But is it likely that in a country where the land is divided, and the number of farmers is great, the majority will ever be educated in colleges, and upon strict scientific principles ? I am ready to answer that such an expectation seems to me a mere delusion. The great body of young farmers must be educated by the example and practices of their elders, by their own efforts at individual and mutual improvement, and by the influence of agricultural journals, books, lecturers, and the example of thoroughly educated men. And, as thoroughly educated men, lecturers, journals, and books of a proper character, cannot be furnished without the aid of scientific schools and thorough culture, the farmers, as a body, are interested in the establishment of all institutions of learning which promise to advance any number of men, however small, in the mysteries of the profession; but, when we design a system of education for a class, common wisdom requires us to contemplate its influence upon each individual. The influence of a single college in any state, or in each state of this Union, would be exceedingly limited; but local societies and travelling lecturers could make an appreciable impression in a year upon the agricultural population of any state, and in New England the interest in the subject is such that there is no difficulty in founding town clubs, and making them at once the agents of the government and the schools for the people.

In the plan indicated, I have, throughout, assumed the disposition of the farmers to educate themselves. This assumption implies a certain degree of education already attained; for a consciousness of the necessity of education is only developed by culture, learning, and reflection. Such being the admitted fact, it remains that the farmers themselves ought at once to institute such means of self-improvement as are at their command. They are, in nearly every state of this Union, a majority of the voters, and the controlling force of society and the government; but I do not from these facts infer the propriety of a reliance on their part upon the powers which they may thus direct. However wisely said, when first said, it is not wise to "look to the government for too much;" and there can be no reasonable doubt of the ability of the farmers to institute and perfect such measures of self-education as are at present needed. But the spirit in which they enter upon this work must be broad, comprehensive, catholic. They will find something, I hope, of example, something of motive, something of power, in their experience as friends and supporters of our system of common school education; and something of all these, I trust, in the facts that this system is kept in motion by the self-imposed taxation of the whole people; that all individuals and classes of men, forgetting their differences of opinion in politics and religion, rally to its support, as being in itself a safe basis on which may be built whatever structures men of wisdom and virtue and piety may desire to erect, whether they labor first and chiefly for the world that is, or for that which is to come.

www.ingramcontent.com/pod-product-compliance
Lightning Source LLC
LaVergne TN
LVHW010144110826
845151LV00002B/422

* 9 7 8 1 4 2 5 5 3 9 0 9 2 *